Risking

Have you got what it takes?

Risking It All

Have you got what it takes?

Martin Webb

RANDOM HOUSE
BUSINESS BOOKS

Published by Random House Business Books in 2005

2 4 6 8 10 9 7 3 5 1

Copyright © 2005 Martin Webb

First published in the United Kingdom by
Random House Business Books in 2005

Random House Business Books
The Random House Group Limited
20 Vauxhall Bridge Road, London SW1V 2SA

Random House Australia (Pty) Limited
20 Alfred Street, Milsons Point, Sydney,
New South Wales 2061, Australia

Random House New Zealand Limited
18 Poland Road, Glenfield, Auckland 10, New Zealand

Random House (Pty) Limited
Isle of Houghton, Corner Boundary Road &Carse O'Gowrie,
Houghton 2198, South Africa

The Random House Group Limited Reg. No. 954009
www.randomhouse.co.uk

A CIP catalogue record for this book is available from the British Library

ISBN 1 8441 3610 8

Papers used by The Random House Group Limited are natural, recyclable products made from wood grown in sustainable forests. The manufacturing processes conform to the environmental regulations of the country of origin

Typeset in Rotis Sans Serif and Sabon

Design and make-up by Roger Walker

Printed and bound in the United Kingdom by
Mackays of Chatham Ltd, Chatham, Kent

Contents

Acknowledgements

Risking It All has been a most exciting project to work on, not least because of the personalities and skills of the people I have had the privilege to meet.

My thanks, then, to all the folk at Ricochet, the directors, the camera and sound operators and, of course, the hugely important producers. My particular thanks to Jane Thorogood who must be one of the best organisers you could hope to find. Jane patiently dealt with all the completely unreasonable demands that I, and other people, made on her.

My thanks also to Ken Langdon, whose wit and wisdom made such a contribution to this book.

And, finally, to my inspiration for all of this – Jack Buster Brett.

Introduction

They say that you need plenty of luck to make a business work and I agree. But you also have to make your own luck, through meticulous planning, intelligent analysis of your marketplace and loads and loads of plain hard work.

You've also got to make some sacrifices. People don't always realise when they set up on their own that they can wave goodbye to holidays, days off and a regular social life for a while. A job is a job, but running a business is a lifestyle. It's best to recognise that before you start. And then there's discipline. Discipline is essential for a successful business. If you're not going to be able to force yourself to do that VAT return on a sunny Sunday afternoon when your mates have asked you down the pub, then forget it. It's self-discipline of course; by definition, there's no one there to force you to do anything.

So why, if all this is true, do I and so many other people repeatedly want to get on to such a grinding path? A path that leads, sometimes, to financial success and total job satisfaction, and other times to failure, with its attendant money problems and blows to your self-esteem.

Well, I've spent my entire career thinking up, setting up and managing businesses. Most have been successful, and the ones that went wrong at least taught me a lot of very good lessons. And here's as near as I can get to explaining why I continue to do it. For me, there's simply nothing like the buzz of knowing a business plan is actually working. It's what gets me up in the morning. It's not the money that motivates me – it's the pure adrenalin rush of knowing that all the planning, worry and hard work are actually paying off. It's such a relief if it's been a hard slog. And, of course, the great thing about running a business is that there's no boss, no career structure and nothing to hold you back but your ability and desire to succeed. If you're hungry enough, you can achieve absolutely anything.

So in this book I've tried to offer the lessons I've learnt from 22 years of running businesses. Thus there's a bit of theory in it; bits that I've come to realise you've just got to understand if your business is going to fly. But it's mainly practical, using 'war stories' not just from my experience, but also from the experiences of the businesses featured in the *Risking It All* Channel 4 film. From all of that, I should be able to cover most of the questions that you want to ask if you're about to embark on your dream of having your own business. And perhaps one or two that you didn't know you needed to ask.

I've organised the book into fairly short chapters, so you can quickly find the bit you need as you plan and open your first premises and start trading. It should help you in the first place to change your dream into a going concern. From there, it goes on to look at the other side of being your own boss – following the entrepreneurial dream of opening more and more outlets, perhaps acquiring businesses and probably selling some from time to time, like cashing in some chips.

So whether you just want to run a village shop, or if your dream is to own an internationally branded chain of British chip shops, this book should help. I hope you find that the advice offered by the contributors to *Risking It All*, and the tales that come from my experience, give you some tips and techniques that bring your dream just that bit closer.

Over the years, I've slowly but surely defined the five areas that you need to look at as you set about planning your dream business. They are:

1 Is the idea **viable?**

You'd be amazed at some of the absolutely crackpot ideas that have stirred people into starting the most surprising businesses; so I start with a look at how you can quickly ascertain if the business of your dreams could possibly fly.

2 Now you need to examine your **motivation** in going it alone.

It's got to be positive as well as negative, such as getting away from what you're doing now. So use the chapters in this section to take an honest look at yourself and define what you're trying to do and why you're trying to do it.

3 Then there's the question of **skills**.

Have you got the necessary ones? I've included those that I've found essential in this section.

4 Then you need the **money** to get going.

Where's that going to come from? There are pros and cons to many different sources of funds and it's best to consider them all carefully.

5 The last thing I look for when assessing a businessperson and their likelihood of success is the **'X factor'**.

Do you have the intuition to act like an entrepreneur or the nous to think quickly enough?

Anyway, I wish you the best of luck, and, as I said at the beginning, you're going to need a dollop of that.

Just a minute, an internationally branded chain of British chip shops... Mmm that one might have legs. Where's the back of a fag packet? I feel a business plan coming on.

Who is Martin Webb?

What others say about Martin

The TV directors who produced the *Risking It All* series worked very closely with Martin as he looked at the businesses that were the dreams of the would-be entrepreneurs.

The directors, camera people and sound recorders visited each business about 32 times over the course of six months to a year. Martin joined them and talked to the business owners six times. The directors, therefore, not only got to know Martin and his methods very well; but they also saw the impact he had on the risk takers; so there's no one better to describe Martin and his skills. Here are some comments from the five of them. In brackets are the names of the programmes that they created.

Emma Clarke (Loaf): 'I was struck by his ability to go into a business and understand it straightaway. He has a massive knowledge of the retail and service industries. The risk takers welcomed the advice he gave because it always seemed to be directed at the heart of a problem or opportunity. But it wasn't just his understanding of the various businesses, but also the speedy way he summed up the personalities of the people he was talking to. He treated them all differently, and unlike many gurus didn't insist, for example, on his ideas for documenting a business plan being the only route to success. On the contrary, he encouraged people to find a method of working that suited them and to stick to it, whether it was a full-blown computerised plan or the back of an envelope.

And yet under his laissez-faire good humour there lurks his meticulous attention to detail. On the cost side, for example, he does insist that everything is costed in, from obvious expenses such as the commissions paid to staff, right down to the things other people often forget about, such as the free coffee in the reception area.

And then he impressed me by demonstrating the difference between the entrepreneur and the person running a business. He believes that if a business is doing well, it's no time for a risk taker to rest on their laurels; it's time to shift up a gear and move on. 'If you're making that amount of money why don't you open up another outlet and go for more,' is definitely his entrepreneurial philosophy.

Nick Hudson (Sejuice and Flying Fortress): I genuinely think he cares, and he empathises very well with people. He's also realistic, and I get the feeling he'd never ask anyone to do anything that he wouldn't be comfortable doing himself. He can also encourage, and he isn't afraid of putting himself on the line or owning up to mistakes he's made. No business guru is untouchable, but some like to think they are. Martin's not in that box.

Jeremy Lee (Octoply): Martin is very clear in the advice that he gives. He doesn't couch his thoughts in management theory, but rather cuts to the nub of the problem and gives practical advice quickly enough to make a difference. The people he was advising really appreciated what he was saying. He didn't pull any punches; when he saw that something was wrong he was quick to point it out.

He talks common sense, to be honest, but it's incredibly useful because he's so good at seeing a business in the context of the big picture. Not only that, but he's a nice guy. He doesn't sound like a big shot entrepreneur, bullying people to see the world his way. He's more the type of guy you'd be glad to have a beer with and explain how your business is faring.

Jane Gerber (<u>Mooch@76</u> and Duke & Co): First of all, Martin looks at a business and immediately sees what's wrong. His forecast of what's going to happen is uncannily accurate. But he always speaks positively. He never points out a flaw without suggesting a solution. And it's not just the humdrum day-to-day problems of running a small business; he also sees the wider angle of how the business might go in the long term. Not only that, but he can connect the two – he connects what's happening now with what is the potential for the future. He uses his experience to help people in the short term with the long term in mind.

Molly Mathieson (Blue Vinny and Reklava): Martin's very easy-going and easy to work with, that's what the risk takers really liked about him. The thing that surprised me about such a successful entrepreneur is his compassion for the people setting up the businesses. He wasn't obsessed with business, he wasn't entirely devoted to the bottom line, but he did genuinely care about how the businesses would fare.

He's very bright, and this helps him to get to what's wrong with a business in no time flat. His advice is not just hard business sense. He makes practical suggestions, too, such as you shouldn't make the portions in the restaurant so huge, a big temptation for chefs, as they impact your profits and stop the customers having a second course and another bottle of wine. But he also pays attention to the soft skills involved in running a successful restaurant, such as training the waitresses; after all they're your ambassadors and you need them to do not just a good job but a great one.

It's not solely running the business that he helps people with either. He's very good on getting the right location for your premises. He hates false economies that threaten your dream business, for example a cheap rental in the wrong place.

In short, he's a very professional businessman with a very human face.

Martin's career

Martin was born in 1964 in London, but was educated at a grammar school in Lancashire. From there he went to Brighton University, where he graduated in business studies. He had to pay his way through college by running disco nights in local clubs and promoting bands. His parents were not sure what to make of this entrepreneurial side to their son, but have been wholly supportive throughout his career.

In 1987, he set up a design company that proved to be unsuccessful and closed in 1992. He believes that the massive learning curve of a fairly spectacular failure made the biggest contribution to him finding out how to set up and run thriving businesses.

In 1993, Martin founded C-Side Ltd with his business partner, Simon Kirby. They started the company on a budget of £10,000, which they scraped together by, for example, Martin holding three jobs dj-ing in clubs four nights a week and running their credit cards up to the limit. Originally just one bar, which they refitted on a shoestring, the business rapidly expanded. Luckily, or perhaps because they anticipated the local mood, the bar caught the imagination of the student population and things took off. In 1998, C-Side was featured in the *Sunday Times* Fast Track 100 as one of the UK's companies with the fastest-growing profits.

Expansion continued at the rate of about one new site every six months. By 2001, when they sold the company, turnover was £20 million and the bottom line profit was £2.3 million. They sold the company to a venture capital company for £15 million. At that point C-Side operated 28 sites, including the famous Zap and Funky Buddha Lounge clubs.

By 1999, he was the founding director of Brighton radio station Surf 107, and, in 2000, became a director of the 'Place to Be', the steering group of Brighton's successful bid to achieve the status of a city. Also in 2000, the national leisure magazine *Theme* awarded him the accolade 'Most Influential Individual'.

This released him to achieve another dream. He spent two years travelling, including walking the famous Inca Trail in Peru. He also used the time in Sydney to learn to skipper a yacht on coastal and cross-Channel passages and became a Royal Yachting Association Yachtmaster. He topped it off by becoming reasonably proficient in French.

Then in May 2004, Martin wanted to combine getting back into the pub business with his desire to put something back into the community. He had some experience in charitable work, having set up Project Safehouse in 2002, a five-bedroomed house that acts as a refuge for at-risk young people, and so decided to set up People's Pubs – the first pub company in the UK to give its entire profit to local charities.

He keeps his commercial hand in with two other pub companies in London that he plans to expand in terms of opening new outlets. Sites include the Medicine Bars in Islington and Shoreditch. He also recently launched Dekorart, a web-based fine art digital printing company with an art gallery in Brighton.

His next big venture is to launch a country sports centre, based in a French château, offering horse riding, clay pigeon shooting, quad biking and other outdoor pursuits. It's quite a challenge to face a major refit of a building in a foreign country; but he says he's enjoying it.

For his own sport, he's a transatlantic yachtsman, having sailed his own yacht from Brighton to Barbados in 2002 and he's currently training to become a pilot.

The risk takers

Lots of people dream of having their own business and of doing something they feel passionate about. They all dream of running a successful business, and some of them have another dream of getting rich. Most people, however, don't even try.

So I take my hat off to the risk takers who were the key contributors to *Risking It All*. Here's who they are.

The business: Blue Vinny

The risk takers

Steve Butcher (36) was an operation line manager manufacturing toilet paper for Kimberly Clark, one of the major players in the area. Lindsay McNally (35) was an human resources manager for the same company. Steve had a great salary, £50k a year, and a company car, but he'd hated every minute of the last three years in his job.

The dream

When he was made redundant, Steve decided to follow the dream he'd had for the last 10 years – starting a high-class restaurant from scratch. The two of them bought an old antiques shop in a quiet village in Kent. Neither had any experience of the restaurant business, and Steve had only ever cooked for family and friends. The food they serve is Modern English using fresh quality produce.

They say 'We're up to our eyeballs in debt.'

At the beginning Lindsay's salary didn't cover all living expenses, so things have been tight. They say they're not doing it for the money, but for the passion; however, if it doesn't work out they'll have to go back to the lives they hated. Lindsay has now left her job and joined the business.

From a 'no knowledge' starting position they're having to learn fast, admitting cheerfully that they don't really know what they're doing. But Steve has given up a very good job and lifestyle to pursue a dream; he's very stubborn and refuses to give in. They opened in December 2004.

The business details

Blue Vinny
The Old Bakery
High Street
Elham
Kent CT4 6TB

Tel: 01303 840835
bluevinny@aol.com
www.bluevinnyrestaurant.co.uk

The business: Mooch

The risk takers

Lee Saunders (28) worked in marketing cigarettes, gambling and alcohol for a small company called Ignis. Paul Ground (32) was a training manager at a company manufacturing stationery and other paper products called Antallis and had been working on a new computer package.

The dream

They want to set up a café/wine bar, with the emphasis on coffee/food by day, and a relaxing, stylish bar at night. They reckoned that Burgess Hill is notorious for its lack of nightlife and that it needed a bar for people of a certain age.

Paul says 'It's a monumental risk and I try not to think about it too much – or I'd cry.'

They both gave up secure jobs and stretched themselves to the limit, remortgaging their houses, putting in all their savings and taking on a big bank loan. They've also got friends and colleagues to invest money. Lee is moving to the area to make the business work. It's going to be completely new to them; neither of them have any experience in the hospitality industry.

The business details

Mooch @ 76
76 Church Walk
Burgess Hill
West Sussex RH15 9AS

Tel: 01444 244888
mooch76cafebar@aol.com
www.mooch76.co.uk

The business: Flying Fortress

The risk takers

Violaine Roberts (37) has been a housewife for 18 months. Andrew Roberts (41) has been a courier for three years. They have four children, two boys Daniel and Jordan (who are 11 and ten) and two girls Chloë and Shannon (aged eight and four).

The dream

Violaine has always wanted to run a family business and dreams that the Flying Fortress will pass from generation to generation. The enterprise, her dream for the last three and a half years, is a family entertainment centre, based on an old airfield in Ford, West Sussex.

Violaine says 'With four children of my own and nowhere close to take them to in the holidays, I knew there was a real need in the community for this type of facility. I wanted to do something about it.'

The family entertainment centre has a large, four-tier play frame in the shape of an aeroplane, which they shipped over from Canada. In time, there will be a cafeteria area with seating for 300 people. They intend to serve everything from drinks and snacks to full meals. Children can hold their birthday parties there and party areas are provided. The premises can hold up to 1000 people.

One of the unique attributes of the centre is that it caters for children of all ages. This means that the local mums can bring the whole family to the one spot. Once a child has paid, they can use the facilities all day.

The business details

Flying Fortress
Northern Grainstore
Ford Airfield
Ford
Arundel
West Sussex BN18 0HY

Tel: 01903 733550
www.flying-fortress.co.uk
captain@flying-fortress.co.uk

The business: Duke & Co

The risk takers

Ben Couldrige (27) was an airline sales manger and Gray Duke (32) an estate agent in Mayfair, London.

The dream

To set up a combined male grooming retail outlet and treatment rooms in the West End of London.

They say 'The concept of the combined facility is totally unique and if we don't do it now someone else will.'

Ben and Gray were both fed up with the constraints of their jobs and felt they needed to be more creative and face a new challenge. It has taken them 18 months to raise the finances, which they described as one of the hardest and most challenging processes they've ever gone through. Ben and Gray are incredibly enthusiastic about this project, despite the length of time it has taken them to get this far. They continue to be very motivated and energetic. They both really need to make this work, as they have borrowed money from their parents, sold belongings and taken out loans. They have a very tight budget and are watching every penny very carefully.

The business details

Duke & Co
Tel: 07843 525 251
Tel: 07921 251 250
info@dukeandco.co.uk
www.dukeandco.co.uk

The business: Reklava

The risk takers

James Cotty (28) has been in engineering for the last 12 years and Kate Cotty (27) has worked as an IT contractor for four years.

The dream

To set up a shop selling design-led gift items. They will be offering a lifestyle concept. The products will include interior/exterior home furnishings, jewellery, acrylic coffee and occasional tables, mirrors and artwork. They're also going to stock Ferrari-branded merchandise.

They say 'We envisage the business challenging the traditional concepts of a shop by offering a range of products and services that are not available elsewhere.'

James and Kate are childhood sweethearts and have been together for ten years. They got married last year. They wanted a lifestyle change and are selling their house and relocating back to their home town of Romsey to live with Kate's mum. They are planning to have a family in the future and are aiming to create a stable environment in which they will have time to enjoy their children. They are both very enthusiastic about running their own business. They are looking forward to the freedom of working for themselves and being able to be much more creative.

The business details

Reklava
14 High Street
Lyndhurst
Hampshire SO43 7BD

Tel: 02380 283666
enquiries@reklava.com
www.reklava.com

The business: Sejuice

The risk takers

Sarah Mulheron worked in the pharmaceutical industry for seven years, the last four as a training manager. Her husband Steven is an engineer in the same industry.

The dream

Sejuice is a new concept in juice bars reflecting Sarah and Steve's passion for freshly made soups, smoothies, shakes, salads and juices. They'll also provide a range of booster shots – from energy shots to hangover cures – designed to help people get the most from their day, whatever else is happening.

Sarah says 'Realistically, I don't think we will be able to draw any salaries from the business for the first six months.'

Sarah has always wanted to run a business and sees Sejuice as a way to share some of their delicious, nutritious soups, smoothies and salads with people who would like to take more control over their health, lives and energy levels but don't have the time to cook. They have re-mortgaged their flat in Horsham to raise the money and moved to Brighton. They have some savings that they'll use to live off for the first six months of trading.

The business details

Sejuice
56 Gardner Street
The North Laines
Brighton BN1 1UN

getfruity@sejuice.uk.com
www.sejuice.uk.com

The business: Loaf

The risk takers

Richard Darlow is a hairdresser and his drinking pal, Craig Wilson, was a carpet fitter.

The dream

They wanted to set up a new hairdressing salon in Woodseats, south Sheffield. Loaf will provide haircutting and colouring, with seven hair stations and one nail station.

They say 'We're going to offer city centre styling in the suburbs.'

Richard and Craig have been friends since school and have known one another for nearly 20 years. Richard is the creative one. He is in charge of the practical side of cutting hair. Craig is the more business-minded one. He will deal with the finances, order stock, work on reception, market the salon and look into future possibilities. Although Craig is putting in all the money, they consider themselves to be equal partners. They hope to be opening more salons in a year, and are also keen to begin developing their own 'Loaf' range of grooming and cosmetic products.

The business details

Loaf
2–4 Meadow Head
Woodseats
Sheffield S8 7UD

Tel: 01114 2359966
www.loafhair.com

The business: Octoply

The risk takers

Nithin, 32 years old and a freelance microbiologist and his sister Neema, 30 and a legal consultant have left their jobs to set up their dream venture.

The dream

Nithin and Neema Rai are aiming to offer a completely new, luxury way of navigating the Thames from Woolwich to Tower Bridge. They bought their Swedish boat in Glasgow, where it's undergoing a full refurbishment.

They say 'It will be an innovative river service that integrates charter, transport, learning and social activities onboard a glass-domed ferry plying the Thames.'

The business details

Octoply
34 Armstrong Road
Royal Arsenal
Woolwich
London SE18 6SW

Tel: 07843 264
http://www.octoply.co.uk

Part 1: Viability

First off, make sure that your idea has got legs. Can you really envisage people buying in large numbers what you're going to sell? Remember, just because it's your passion it doesn't mean that it's everyone else's.

Before you embark on an expensive business set-up, go through some basic rules that govern whether it's a viable idea or not. A dream is a dream, and it's your initiative that's going to turn it into reality; but if you can't persuade a few people to agree that the project has potential you could be dreaming with your head in the clouds rather than, as is businesslike, with both feet firmly planted on the ground.

Chapter 1 You've got to talk to potential customers; in marketing parlance 'do your market research'. Get a picture in your head of what the premises will look like and what you're offering inside, and test it out by talking to potential customers. Look very hard, too, at the competition in the area around your potential premises.

Chapter 2 Now take care that it's not just your passion. This is quite tricky. You've got to have passion for what you're about to do in terms of really believing that people will love what you're offering as much as you do; but don't let that passion blind you to the evidence around you. If you absolutely love Spanish embroidery, that's great. But it's not necessarily a business. And if you think there's an opportunity in a location for a Spanish embroidery boutique, ask yourself a hard question – why has no one in this area done it before?

Chapter 3 All businesses need a plan. Now, I don't have a special formula for that plan, and I do think that everyone should work out their own way of evolving a plan and putting it down on paper. But you've got to start by thinking it through before you jump in, and certainly before you spend a brass farthing on the project.

Chapter 4 When you have an idea, particularly if you've had it for quite a while, it can be easy for it to grow on you until it seems a compelling case. But could a sensible third party easily knock it down? That's why I've put in this section how essential it is to have someone to talk to about the idea openly and honestly. You need to bounce it off someone who wants the idea to fly but can add a second opinion on where the flaws may lie. This doesn't mean that their job is to kill the project; rather it means that their suggestions could make the difference between a viable idea and the one you first thought of.

Chapter 5 It may seem a bit odd to put break-even analysis, a financial technique, into a section about overall viability, but it's such a major indicator of the feasibility of a business plan that it's one of the first techniques you've got to master.

Chapter 6 The most difficult part of running a business is probably getting the right people to work in it and motivating them to give of their best. After all, you feel passionate about what you're doing because it's your idea and you're hoping to make a lot of money out of it. How do you motivate people to share that passion but only earn a normal living out of it?

Chapter 7 Imagine you're building a brand. What are the risks involved, and when is the right time to sell the brand on?

Chapter 8 If you want to get ahead get organised. There are three ways to run a retail business – unprofessionally, professionally and ultra-professionally. Make sure you're in the third category.

Once you've exposed your idea to all of these questions, you'll have a very clear insight into whether your idea's got legs or not.

1 At first glance, will the business fly?

Budding entrepreneurs sometimes get carried away with their own excitement at the prospect of being their own boss and of trying to make a small fortune, well, small at least to start with. This may set them off on a course that a bit more thought might have shown to be a non-starter. Keep your feet on the ground, think about your idea and make sure it is not only brilliant, but also viable.

Don't try to push water up a hill

You know the old sayings, 'They've got the gift of the gab', 'They could sell fridges to the Eskimos or white suits to an undertaker'. Well let them try. It's a lot easier to check in as many ways as possible that an idea is viable before you make the big leap. Look, you wouldn't set up a second-hand clothes shop in Bond Street would you, and you wouldn't run a beer tent at a Salvation Army meeting. So why would you locate your new business in an area where the passing or local trade doesn't give you the type of person you know will be attracted to your premises and your products? OK, in the end people might travel miles to eat at your restaurant or dance in your club, but in the early stages there's got to be a fairly ready local market that you can tap into to get you going.

In My Experience: Get the strength of some research behind your instincts

Hunches are all well and good, but you need to back them up with research and facts. It's always easier to start to spend money implementing your dream business plan than to meticulously check that there's a ready market. Make sure you haven't committed yourself to expenditure by following your instincts.

I see many examples of new businesspeople who believe that they can 'create a local market' by changing the habits that the local people have built up over years and make them spend their money differently. I get concerned when someone says, 'There's got to be a market for it here, the nearest competitor is miles away.' It makes me ask why no one else has done it here. How can you be the first person to think that this idea will work in this location?

Strange as it may seem, I'm more comfortable when there are outlets with a pretty similar idea to yours operating quite nearby. OK, probably next door is a little close, but if they're miles away, perhaps the market is too. Starting a business is struggle enough without having to introduce a totally new concept to a sceptical local market.

In My Experience: It's actually easier to reinvent the wheel in the retail business than to think of a new method of transport

It's amazing how often it's the third owner of a business who actually makes money. The first owners spend the capital to set it up and perhaps struggle enough to get it to break even. But they're in debt, so, after an exhausting period of time and at huge expense, they sell the business for nearly enough to pay off the debt to someone who wants to own the outlet for as little time as possible. They mean to repair the finances, perhaps spend the little extra bit of money the original owners couldn't find and build a reasonably viable business. After a short time, perhaps months rather than years, they sell it at a reasonable profit to a company that has a number of similar outlets and knows that they can make good money out of this one in the long term.

We can learn from this. It might be that the best way to get going is to act like the second owner in this example, and buy an existing outlet that you know you can improve with money and your skills. Then get it going reasonably well and move on by selling it and starting again, or buying another one to start your own chain. At least it ensures that the idea is viable.

Look, I'm not saying you can't start from scratch, of course you can; but in the planning stages don't assume that this is your only entry point.

Do your homework

So how do you check the viability of your idea? How do you make sure that where you're setting up offers you a good chance of attracting people and that this is the right time to have a go? You need a strategy – what are you going to sell, to whom are you going to sell it and how are you going to set about doing it?

In retail and service businesses generally, identifying the right premises is a good starting point. Remember the old estate agent maxim, the value of a property depends on three things – location, location and location. Find a possible location and then study the passing trade or footprint. Are they old or young, rich or poor, busy or with time on their hands, trendy or conservative? You get the picture. Do your research in the mornings, afternoons and evenings of different days of the week. Take notes so that you can document your potential market when the time comes. Right, so that, at least to begin with, is whom you've got to sell to.

Now look at what they buy at present. What shops or outlets operate in the area? Check that they're successful, first by looking at how busy they seem to be at the times you would expect them to be and then by asking the people running the businesses, preferably each owner. Listen carefully to what they say. You'll probably get a truthful answer, but beware of overenthusiasm such as 'It's a gold mine'; people use exaggeration to mask panic.

More useful terms to hear are, 'Rushed off our feet' and 'Really well and much better than last year'. These are positive and have the ring of truth. Terms such as 'Pretty good, but we're just waiting for the summer, the election [or any other impending event]' sound dodgy and possibly a whistle in the dark. It's not difficult to understand how things are going. This is particularly true if you talk to junior people, to whom the business only means a short-term way of earning their living, as well as the owner. This research work should give you a fair idea of how well your product or service might sell.

Now look at the appearance of the competitive or near competitive premises. Study particularly the obviously successful ones. The footprint obviously likes that kind of place, so it could be the starting point of how you fit out your outlet and how you sell your product to the market. All you've got to do is make sure that you do it in a similar way but better.

What the business schools say...

In theory you should use market researchers, people who organise focus groups to test out your idea and that sort of thing. They gather a lot of data and offer lots of possible and weighted interpretations of the data.

But...

Quite honestly, I think your observation and opinion are at least as good without going to that trouble and expense. I'd rather spend that kind of budget on public relations or advertising and promotion.

From the
TV Series

The right time and the right place

The play centre is a great example of someone getting this sort of pre-thinking right. It's set up in an area where lots of reasonably well-off middle-class people live, work and send their kids to school. The number of single-parent families is growing and everyone is looking for fun places to take their children. The children themselves are used to a high level of entertainment and frequently get bored if they feel they have nothing to do.

The area is obviously ripe for the unusual type of fun that the Flying Fortress offers. Violaine had spotted this, asked her friends and contacts at the school gate and confirmed that, were it available, the aeroplane-based playground would be well used.

In My Experience: Seeing the business from the customers' point of view

I try to put myself into the shoes of a possible buyer. If I were that sort of person would I go in? Would I use this business if I were a member of the public? Can I imagine this business with queues around the block? It's a question of trying to visualise the business being successful. There's more about this gut feeling in the section of the book dealing with the X-factor.

2 Make sure there's a market for your passion

Making money, particularly in the early stages of a new idea, is a serious business; there's no place for your passionate feel-goods or deep-felt hang-ups. Ask yourself, and maybe someone else who knows you, if any big decision you're about to make is realistic or emotional.

Everybody's different; make sure your market shares your passion

Look, you've started the business with a vision of something you want to do. I know you're passionate about taking your new concept to market and bursting for people to love your products and services as much as you hoped they would. But, whatever your motivation for getting into this, it's time to remind yourself about the real reason for going into business – making money. OK, OK, I know you want to have fun running your own thing; but, believe me, there's no fun in running a business that's not making money.

You've got to look at your passion for the product and service you're dying to sell with a dispassionate marketing person's hat on. Do other people want the same thing? Is there a market for your product however good it is and however much you think that people damn well should want it?

The best way to look at this is to imagine that there is no such thing as a product unless there is a market for it and vice versa.

In My Experience: Why has no one done it before?

I've seen a business start up where the facts were these: there were 40 players already in the service business that they were going to offer, but there hadn't been a new one started up in the last ten years. Why not?

Now, even if they were offering a very different service with additional facilities and so on, they still needed to ask the question, 'Why has no one from the 40 businesses with experience of this trade tried such a thing before?' You can't assume there's a market just because no one has done it before. That particular start-up looked, frankly, like a very big risk.

Product/markets

Try not to think solely in terms of products and services without at the same time considering the market for them. Don't plan to stock a product or offer a service if you can't easily identify the people who will want to buy them and your ability to get to them. Don't set up shop until you're sure that the current footprint outside your shop, that is the people who already pass by, includes a sufficient number who will want to come into the shop and buy products.

Let's think about a famous case of an entrepreneur ruining his own business by ignoring this product/market rule. Gerald Ratner set up a chain of cut-price or low-price jewellery and tableware. The Ratner name was once a nationwide fixture on British high-streets, but Mr Ratner effectively killed the company in 1991 with a speech to the Institute of Directors, when he joked that one of his firm's products was 'total crap', and boasted that some of its earrings were 'cheaper than a prawn sandwich'.

The speech, instantly seized upon by the media, wiped an estimated £500m from the value of the company and put an end to a successful and rising brand.

Mr Ratner left the firm the following year, and his name was expunged from the company in 1994.

Let's start with the question, 'Were the products total crap?' In the eyes of Mr Ratner they were. His taste, we are led to believe, was for much more upmarket products with a sound provenance, such as Fabergé and Aspreys, and a price ticket massively above the ones you found in Ratner. But he had already proved that there was a big market for low-priced jewellery in his stores. The product is not total crap if someone with a low disposable income who wants to have a decanter and six sherry glasses and can actually buy them. OK, everyone knows that if the decanter and glasses sold for £14, they wouldn't be the same as the ones they use for state banquets at Windsor Castle and that the earrings might last for less time than a prawn sandwich; but people wanted to buy them. There was a product/market and Gerald Ratner forgot about that. By describing the products in such dreadful terms he insulted his market. His emotional feelings about his products, and perhaps his wish for a cheap laugh from his fellow fat-cat directors, cost him dear.

What the business schools say...

The business schools want you to 'believe in your products and what you're doing'. They teach that committed people are more likely to be successful than others who take a more dispassionate view.

But...

Yes and no, it's a balance. I'd always back the business person taking a long cold look at their prospects for making money against the enthusiastic inventor who thinks they've got it right and that anyone who doesn't agree with them is wrong and can go hang. But you do need to believe in what you're doing. You need to believe that your objective is a good one – to take on a product/market, nurture it, grow it and get a good return on your investment. Oh, and you probably want to feel proud of what you've done when it's all over.

Incidentally, I don't mean to suggest in this chapter that you should ignore intuition and passion. What I am saying is that you should tune your intuition not to think about innovation in product terms, or in terms of a new market; but tune it to think about the link between the product and the market. Keep asking yourself, 'What is my strategy? What am I trying to sell and to whom am I trying to sell it?'

From the TV Series

Stocking presents that are just what you've always wanted

James, who in his gift shop, Reklava, aimed at the top end of the tourist market in the New Forest, is a Ferrari nut.

Indeed, one of the reasons he went for his own business was to be able to buy the Ferraris and Ferrari paraphernalia that he loves. He's incredibly knowledgeable about the marque. He can explain how they're built, what the latest model has in it and so on. If a similar enthusiast were to come into the shop they would, the pair of them, be as happy as a keen gardener talking to the head person at Kew Gardens.

Now, that would be OK if James had not let this emotional wish affect the stock that he bought for the shop. But just in case, I suppose, such an enthusiast came into the shop, he bought everything from Ferrari tie-pins, to Ferrari baseball hats to Ferrari CD holders. Like a kid in a sweet shop, he found himself suddenly able to buy exactly what he wanted, in large numbers and at wholesale prices.

Now think about Reklava's market. Half of them are women. OK, I know some women are hugely interested in Ferraris, but an awful lot are not. And I could go on. In the end, James is taking up valuable shelf space with a minority interest product for emotional reasons.

When I challenged him about this he mentioned the fact that there was a Ferrari showroom not far from the shop.

In My Experience: Try selling not telling

Associated with this topic is the need, when you are persuading people to come to your outlet and buy, to sell to them rather than tell them all about your products and services.

Let's look at an easy example first to make the point. Have you ever enjoyed buying a computer? A lot of computer salesman are, fortunately, very knowledgeable about quite a complex product. The good ones can listen to your requirements and then describe the features of their products in terms of their way of answering your needs. They say, 'If you have to print out large reports there is probably a good return on an investment in the top model in the range. It'll save you a lot of time.' They don't say, 'This printer has a rear entry sheet feeder that holds about 100 sheets of 64 gram per square metre paper and allows the printer to print at 64 megabytes per second.' You can enjoy buying from the first one; the latter can be a nightmare.

Look at your promotional material with this in mind. Does your passion and knowledge make you put in too much about the detail of the product, and not enough about what it does for the consumer? When you're selling gifts, make your first question, 'Who's it for?' That way you can talk about the how the recipient will enjoy it.

3 Plan, don't jump in

If you're going to succeed in setting up your own business, you've got to get your attitude right, learn as fast as you can from as many sources as are available and think about the timing of what you're doing.

Get your attitude right

When they know that you've set up and grown your own business, other people frequently confide in you their version of the business of their dreams. Often they're doing just that – dreaming – and have no intention of attempting to make it come true. (Indeed some people dream and are on the brink of taking the plunge for so long that you've got to come to the conclusion that they are superglued to the diving board.)

Sometimes, their dream, if they were to implement it, would in fact be a nightmare. (I mean, have you ever really thought through what it's like to run a pub in the country. It would be akin to opening up your living room to the same people every night whether you like them or not. And there are no police and no brewery overlord to enforce the licensing laws, so these people will stay until they want to go. Oh, and your hours are nine in the morning until, say, midnight, and that's on a good day. I'm not knocking it, but be aware of what it will entail.)

What the business schools say...

Business schools preach the good sense of running team-planning sessions. They advocate having a facilitator to help the planning process along. There are many, many processes that a team can go through when they're planning. There are exercises such as 'the obituary', where the team individually writes down what they think the obituaries would say if the company failed. This helps to identify the weaknesses that are in the business at the moment. You can also play management games and spend huge amounts of time 'brainstorming' and 'thinking outside the square'.

But...

All of these techniques have merit, but the trouble is that they can take up too much time for the small business to afford. In the end, planning comes down to three phases. Ask yourself what are the strengths and weaknesses of the business, set objectives for putting the weaknesses right, and then decide on and document an action plan you know to be feasible. Then, jolly well get on and do the actions. Businesses thrive when people are doing things, less so when they're contemplating their navels.

Nonetheless, there are good opportunities for turning a passion into a business. So, if you want to open your art gallery or antiques shop, or if your bent is towards designing and installing kitchens or gardens, there are people who have gone before you and done it. Let's take as an example the dream of opening a shop.

There's no doubt that if your passion is to open an art gallery in Bond Street you'll need a lot of capital and an encyclopaedic knowledge of the international art market. Even then, your lack of experience in the retail business will almost certainly be your, very expensive, downfall. We are not talking mega-corporations here to begin with, rather starting off with one shop in a less than centrally located area of a town or village.

Most dreamers have to make it happen with very little capital. And that seems to be the first clue; you can't achieve your dream in a fortnight. This is a long-term plan and a long-term commitment. Think ten years to the end of the project, not necessarily in terms of a business plan, but rather as a life plan. Where are you going and what do you have to do to get there? Some people say that knowing the exit strategy after the ten-year plan is important, others that such a plan will become clearer as time passes. I'm mainly with the latter; but my partner Simon thinks we should have thought about the exit strategy earlier than we actually did.

Then ask yourself, 'Do I passionately want to do it?' You are going to have to sell things, it's not like working in a chemist shop; it's about getting to know your customers and helping them to buy. Selling requires a passion for the product that rubs off on the customer. That doesn't mean that you're going to have to use high-pressure selling techniques. Putting people under pressure tends, at best, to sell one thing to each person who comes into the shop; but they don't come back. So the thing that sells for you is your commitment, and your knowledge of the product and its benefit to customers. They buy because they trust you when you say, 'This is good, comes from a good source and is right for you.' That's how you build up the essential customer relationships that provide repeat visits and purchases.

So, you've got a life plan and you've made sure you're ready for the inevitable selling part of the job, and you've got your attitude to customers right.

Exploit people already in the know

Right, you've jumped in, or are about to jump in, so your learning curve needs to be very steep. You're going to eat drink and sleep your chosen subject all day every day. You read, you browse the Internet and you learn. It needs to be a fairly narrow field, since you want to be an expert as quickly as you can. A man who set up a gallery to sell prints flirted with sculpture since it was an associated art, but stopped when he realised that his learning time was being spread too thin. You may already be pretty knowledgeable when you start, but look for people who can give you short cuts in making further progress. Lean particularly on anyone who is going to be a supplier to you and pick their brains. They know the business inside out and are somewhat motivated to help you since they want you for a customer. Exploit any other contacts as well; this is no time to be a shrinking violet. Wander into similar places in other areas and talk to the owner. If they don't see you as direct competition they will almost certainly be pleased to help. After all, you would in their place. Oh, and read the trade press avidly.

Quite quickly you'll become hardly aware of how much you really do know. Because you don't realise how much you've learnt, at first you'll be surprised when you find that the person who looks after the shop for one day while you go to a wedding has done so much damage in such a short time. They simply didn't know enough.

In My Experience: Transferring one skill to another application

I know one person who took his skills from his previous working life to an antique stall in Petticoat Lane. He had previously been in the money markets connecting buyers to sellers and depending for his profit on the margin between the two prices. Everyone knew when he started that he knew very little about antiques and wondered how he would survive. The answer was his ability, learnt in the money markets, to remember exactly what he had paid for every individual item on a crowded stall, none of which had a price tag on it. This made him a lethal negotiator, since he always looked very casual and never consulted documents or books. In the end, he became an expert in a narrow field, took on a partner and owned a number of shops.

Get the timing right

You know the water is warm, you are braced for the dive, so what are you waiting for?

In My Experience: Make the market drive the business plan

Some people decide that the service they're offering in their restaurant or whatever will be so different that their business will grow just by word of mouth, so they don't bother getting anyone to take a long hard look at the marketing side.

Think about setting up a water taxi service. It's beautiful to cruise to work and cruise back again when the weather's warm. Indeed, it's probably the nicest place in a big city to be when it's really hot – river breeze and all that. But it's not quite so nice when it's freezing cold and there's a bit of a flood stream running. Apart from anything else, when a strong current's against you, it could make the journey take twice as long.

This is why river passenger traffic goes dead in September and doesn't really come back to life until May or June. This makes it sensible to plan to get such a business started at the beginning of the summer. It would probably be wise to set that date as the project completion date and work back from there. You're trying to make a real understanding of the market drive your business plan.

There is a fundamental rule in business that risk and reward go hand in hand – the higher the risk, the higher the reward, however you measure it. This makes selecting the right time to go for your dream a two-edged sword. Suppose you have a £200,000 mortgage on your property, two children at school and another on the way, and ends are only just meeting on a salary of £55,000 a year; at that time, the risk of your dream making an unwelcome but enforced change to your standard of living is probably too high. But remember those people with superglue on their feet, and don't wait too long. I mean, seriously, if you have enough money from your early retirement package to live comfortably without working at all, are you really going to want to get up six days a week to run a village post office? By then, you've left it too late.

The timing is a matter of capital and resources. It's a question of weighing up your obligations to your dependants, saving enough capital to put some money in as shareholders' funds and going for it as soon as common sense tells you these things are in balance.

A lot of people succeed in getting going by having one partner leaving work and starting the dream, while the other continues earning in their current job, works for the dream during their time off and doesn't draw any money out of the new business. It's a good plan.

Get paid for learning the trade

Paul and Lee knew very little about running a café/bar when they set up Mooch in Burgess Hill. Neither had any experience, they just had an idea of what they wanted to provide as a new idea to the local people. I wondered if they wouldn't have made a better start if at least one of them had got a job in a bar or a café. That way, they would have quickly learnt a lot about what's involved in managing such a business.

4 One plus one equals at least three

Choosing a good business partner is a great way of making up for your lack of business experience. You need someone to bounce ideas off, trust to do some important tasks and perhaps back you up in an argument. Here's how to divide the overall job of the entrepreneur into its two equally important roles.

Balancing the 'here and now' with the 'where are we going?'

In my experience, two people working together can always create more than the sum of what they could do on their own. One of the key ways this works is in striking a balance between handling the pressures and problems of today against the longer-term thinking that you need to build your dream. Two heads are better than one in this area. If you are on your own, you have to divide your head into two parts – the operational, short-term action/reaction part, and the aspirational, long-term strategy part. The problem looks like this:

1 Without a long-term strategy, your company runs the risk that decisions you're making today will have a negative impact on results in the future.

2 But we have to stay real; business people are always under pressure to carry out urgent day-to-day tasks. You have to meet today's sales, you've got to at least break even every month and there are going to be short-term problems to be overcome. It tends to be customers, of course, who drive this; you have to respond to their needs in time to keep them as customers. Everyone in the business is involved in such work and in operational, or short-term, planning. In a fast-moving environment, it's little wonder that planning for the future runs the danger of taking second place.

3 If these two statements are true for all organisations, they are much more dramatically correct in start-ups and small companies. There's no point in defending an action as being right for the long term if it's going to result in the business running out of cash. On the other hand, stocking products, for example, that are way outside the main route you've planned could be catastrophic for the future.

So we come back to the two heads. The top of any start-up company needs someone with a 'can do' and 'do it now' attitude. It needs someone who will discuss a problem, find a solution and immediately pick up the telephone to start implementing it. You can expect some fancy footwork from the person in this role. You've got to be nimble to survive all the day-to-day problems a business throws up. No one has solved the particular problems you're about to face; there is no precedent, so one of the two heads has to spot solutions to problems or opportunities that would be described by some managers in large companies as completely 'off the wall'.

And yet, and yet, no one built a business without thought for the future affecting what we do now – the second head. Some people can simulate the two heads inside their one brain. Reacting, ducking and weaving with the best of them, but also, from time to time, checking that they are not mortgaging the future or adopting short-term measures that endanger the long-term goal. But I recommend forming teams of two, where one person is clearly the go-getter, and the other the 'just a minute, let's think this through, there's another opportunity here' person. So, think on. Can you do it yourself with a Chinese wall in your head separating the two processes or do you need a partner?

Working with Simon

I was extremely fortunate to have Simon as my partner during the years that we built a pub chain, which, in the end, had the equivalent of 250 full-time staff. He came equipped with a degree in maths and computing. He's a meticulous person, who's not scared of detail. So he took on the role of administration and, crucially, managed the properties that we bought or leased. He's also great dealing with the intricacies of people administration and looked after staff issues, keeping us on the right side, for example, of health and safety and other regulatory matters.

This freed me up for my main tasks, building the clientele that came into the bars and finding and designing the next locations. I tended to be in charge of the marketing side and the main person involved in public relations, arranging interviews and events for local and national papers and magazines. Don't get me wrong. We did get involved in each other's side of the business, and, vitally, we both acted as each other's sounding board. We confirmed what we were going to do and occasionally told each other to think something through again. But the fact that we recognised the two roles solved the short-term/long-term problem.

In Simon's words, 'Martin made the sites sell; I made the sites profitable.'

There was another huge benefit in this arrangement in the 'culture' of the organisation. Staff could easily identify the roles that Simon and I were carrying out and could respond to them. On the one hand, they were very conscious of the need for a return on investment. They kept a tight grip on costs and negotiated well with suppliers and so on to meet Simon's strict standards for profitability. On the other hand, they knew that I hated missing an opportunity and they were keen to spot any and follow them through – even if it meant taking a bit of a risk. And that, you could say, was exactly what we wanted the overall attitude of every person in the business to be.

What the business schools say... Is it a straight split, or does someone have the decision-making edge?

Suppose you have decided to go with two people, the next decision is whether the partnership is equal, or if one of the partners is slightly more equal than the other. Some venture capitalists that work with start-ups have come to the conclusion that every team needs an identified leader. They advocate, for example, that the shares in a limited company are not split 50–50, but that one shareholder is given the edge, even if it is only 51–49. That way, they claim, if it becomes necessary to arbitrate between two courses of action they both know in advance whose opinion will hold.

But...

Look, they could be right, but I know two very successful entrepreneurs whose experience is that the 50–50 split can work well. One of them, the long-term thinker of the duo, says that even the smallest edge would have lessened his ability to argue his case, and the 'do it now' merchant would have forced through actions that eventually proved to be mistakes. He went on, however, to reveal that there was an arbiter, or at least another person involved in the decision-making process. This person played the role of non-executive, and low-paid, chairman. During planning sessions, the chairman would force the two people to go through a route of logic that would often reveal to the more impetuous of the two that the way forward he was advocating was not right for the business as a whole. Indeed, this became such a feature of the behaviour of the team that the go-getter would often, at the end of such a discussion, turn on his partner in mock rage saying, 'There you are, I told you it wasn't a good idea' – his way of backing down.

Do you need a third party?

If you are doing the whole thing on your own, make sure you have built in at least a simulation of this arbitration. It doesn't matter who it is, your accountant, your spouse, your eldest child or your bank manager, just have someone in whom you confide and who can tell you to your face that you are about to drop a clanger. (On second thoughts probably not your bank manager. As we will see, they are more concerned with avoiding trouble and potential bad debts than encouraging the green shoots of commerce. If the business takes three years to really get going and prosper, that particular person won't be there to see it happen anyway.)

There are two illuminating stories told about Robert Townsend, the former CEO of Avis. In the first his wife famously made him think about his role as the Director of Strategic Planning in one of his companies by saying, 'And what did you plan today, dear?' In the other, his feisty sidekick, on being told of a rather hairy diversification Townsend was proposing, said, 'I don't know what you call that, but we Poles call it pissing in the soup.' Even the greats need a third party.

From the TV Series

Making beautiful music together

Loaf is a great partnership in this regard. One of them is the creative hairdresser, the other an ex-carpet fitter good with money and an able administrator. In the best partnerships, the whole is definitely greater than the sum of the parts. Neither could do it on their own; but they were drinking mates and they worked out that between them they could do it in fine style.

5 How much do you have to sell to cover your costs?

One of the most important tools for planning your business and monitoring its progress is a financial one – break-even analysis. Here's how to make it work for you.

What does break-even analysis do for us?

An alarming number of people go into business with little or no understanding of the financial side of things. I've spoken to one woman who is setting up a company to sell educational materials to child minders. It seems to me that it's a good idea and very much of its time. When I suggested she draw up a spreadsheet of her costs and estimated revenues, she replied that she just couldn't get her head around figures and was going to leave all that to the accountant. To be honest, I think that's a bit like driving a car and only seeing road signs every six months.

I am quite happy for businesspeople to be uncertain how accountants draw up the annual report from the bookkeeping figures; but I'm also convinced that you've got to be able to understand enough about finance to help with two processes. You need to know enough to use the numbers to help with planning, and to read the signals that the numbers give on your progress. Properly used, they allow you to make the fine-tuning adjustments that allow managers to go from a mediocre performance to a great one. Of these signals, break-even analysis is by far the most important at the beginning of your dream project.

The difference between success and failure in a new business revolves around how long it takes for the business to start making a profit. While you are still spending more money than you're receiving in sales revenues, you remain uncertain whether your dream is going to come true or turn into a nightmare of sleepless nights.

Here's how it works. Every month you are going to spend money, whether anyone comes through the door to buy something or not. These expenses are called, quite reasonably, fixed costs. They include the rental of the premises, insurances, staff costs, maintenance work, marketing costs and so on. As part of your plan, you need to make an absolutely complete list of these. Don't miss anything out, or the calculation will go horribly wrong.

Some businesses only have fixed costs. What this means is that no matter how much revenue comes in, they only have the fixed costs to cover before they reach the break-even point. This gives them a very simple break-even analysis.

In My Experience: Make sure you've worked out the numbers before you make a commitment

Some businesses have no variable costs. A transport business, for example, has to make its scheduled runs and, of course, vehicles use the same amount of fuel whether they're full or empty. The break-even analysis for such a business is therefore quite straightforward.

But I've seen people sign up for vehicles without even doing a break-even analysis. So subsequently when they did work it out, whether they liked the break-even point or not, they were committed into going ahead with buying what they'd contracted for.

It's a bit optimistic to make commitments before you've done the numbers, it looks too much like emotion getting in the way of sound business common sense.

The other costs are called variable costs, and only really occur when a customer buys something. They are the ingredients on the plate in the restaurant, or the cost of the pen in the newsagent. The more you sell, the higher the variable costs, but since you're selling the items for more than you paid for them, the fact that you've got higher variable costs also means that you're making a larger contribution towards your fixed costs and subsequently your profits. People call it all sorts of things, but I find the word contribution fits the bill best. When you have worked out the difference between what customers paid for your products and what you paid for them, you have the *contribution* that the profit on that revenue has made to fixed costs.

Here's the formula in equation form:

$$\text{revenues} - \text{direct costs} = \text{contribution}$$
$$\text{contribution} - \text{fixed costs} = \text{net profit}$$

You will, I'm afraid, hear these terms, and others, to describe the same equation; but it's easy enough to work out what the words mean if you fully understand the concept.

It should be easy enough to know your fixed costs. Don't fool yourself though; if some are slightly uncertain, take the higher end of the possibilities. It's crucial to start from an accurate estimate of these costs. If you guess too high that's better than going the other way. You can always adjust it when you have real experience as the months go by.

The next bit is trickier. You have to make an estimate of the contribution that you'll make when the customers start buying. Let's start with a simple example to make the point. Suppose you were running a pub that sold only Guinness. From your supplier you would know exactly how much each pint that you sell has cost you.

Here's the equation where the selling pint of a price is £3.00 and you buy it in at £1. Your fixed costs are £1,200 per week. The contribution for each pint is £2. So you need to sell 600 (1,200 divided by 2) to cover the fixed costs. So 600 pints is your break-even point.

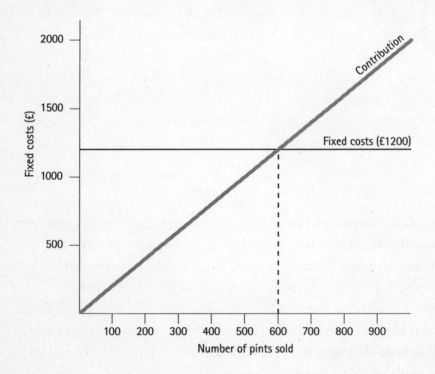

That way it's dead easy; but this Guinness-only scenario is unlikely to be the case because you'll sell all sorts of other drinks too. But if you stick with drinks only, you should be able to estimate the average cost of all the drinks you sell. You can use that figure for planning purposes and adjust it with experience. For example, if your average drinks price for the whole range is £3.50, the average variable cost is £1.50 and your fixed costs have risen to £1,600 per week, then you need to sell 800 drinks (1,600 divided by £2) to cover your costs.

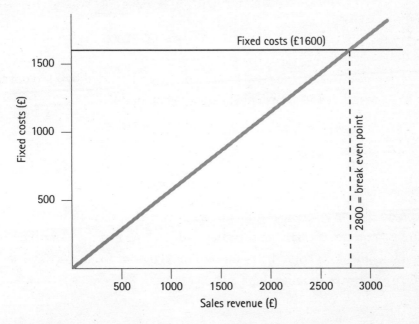

But, of course, you sell food as well, and the margin on food ingredients is very different from that on drinks. Again, you have to make an estimate. Using your common sense, you'll work out a reasonable way of doing it. Perhaps you estimate the ratio of drinks to food that customers will consume. Say, at lunchtime, someone who spends £6 on food is likely to spend £5 on two drinks. In the evening, many people will only drink, but a customer who spends £15 on food may well spend £12 on drinks. And so on.

However you do it, you now have an estimate of the contribution that sales make to fixed costs and profits. Say your best estimate is an overall contribution of 50 per cent, because on average you sell the products for double the price you paid for them. And let's say your monthly fixed costs are £6,000. At what point does the contribution from sales equal the total of your fixed costs? That's your break-even point.

So this example, in equation form, is as follows:

sales	12000
variable costs	6000
gross profit	6000
fixed costs	6000
profit	0

If you do this on a spreadsheet, you can play with it to your heart's content. You can try halving the sales and see how bad the situation could become. You could have another look at your fixed costs and see if there are any economies there and so on.

Using break-even analysis for budgeting

If you've done this exercise you'll find it useful in many ways. First of all, it gives you your budget. This is the estimate of the first year's figures and is essential for your bank manager if you're borrowing money, or for your shareholders if you're trying to attract capital from investors. When you add in the one-off costs of fitting out, you can see how long it takes to recover that money as well.

What the business schools say...

Once you've covered your fixed costs, all additional contribution goes straight to the bottom line.

But...

This is true, but lots of people get caught out when, as a result of rising sales, they hit a sudden rise in fixed costs, because, for example, they have to take someone else on. Make sure that you add into your plan when the fixed costs will take such a leap.

In My Experience: Resigning too soon

Here's an example of a business facing a sudden increase in fixed costs.

It's often sensible for one person in a partnership to stay on at their own job while the other partner gets the new business going. It saves costs and ensures that whatever happens there's at least one salary coming in. But then the person staying in their job is anxious to leave as soon as possible and get on with creating their dream. This eagerness can make them resign just before the business achieves break-even. This basically adds another salary to their overheads and further delays break-even. I think this is a bit risky and that they might be better to wait a while until the business could absorb the extra overhead and still break even.

What the business schools say...

In a pub, the core business is selling drinks. If you can cover your fixed costs from the contribution of the drinks side, then any contribution from food goes directly to the bottom line.

But...

This is pretty well true; and I find the same goes for any core business. For example, you can reverse this if you're running a restaurant whose core attraction is food. Cover your fixed costs with the food and the contribution from drinks goes straight into your pocket.

6 Motivating your people

However well you're motivated yourself, you'll actually start to make real money when you motivate other people to work hard and smart to make your business thrive. Think about each of your key people as an individual and decide roughly how you're going to go about getting the best out of them.

Start with the right kind of person

Ideally, you want people who are charismatic, good with customers and dedicated to providing them with a first-class service. You can motivate such people quite easily. Just make sure that they feel loved. OK, I know that's quite a strong word, but it's the one that comes nearest to what I'm trying to say. They need to feel important and part of the team. Just as you hired them because they smile a lot, so you must smile at them and hold friendly conversations about their lives outside as well as inside work.

And appreciation; you can't overestimate the importance of appreciation. It's a key factor for keeping people working hard and smart. So, try to remember that people work for money but do a bit extra for recognition, praise and reward. If you think someone is doing a good job never forget to tell them. A lot of people leave the big 'thank you' until a task is complete, but it's better to do it all the time when people are working on something and making progress. If for no other reason, you can thank them for doing something that otherwise you would have to do yourself.

Don't always visit your premises at the same time every day. That way you make sure that everyone knows you and expects you to drop in at any time. I've heard it called 'managing by wandering around', and it's very important.

When you're interviewing people, don't just ask about their CV and their experience. A good question is one that helps you to judge whether the person is going to fit into the way your business works – its culture if you like. So a good question is, 'What sort of company do you like working for?' If they use words like 'security', 'one that makes me exactly aware of what I've got to do', this could indicate that they are unlikely to want to take a risk and use their initiative. You can think about your own examples. Try not to hire someone who you know will have to change their way of working to fit in with the rest of your people: they probably won't. Put a lot of time and thought into finding the right people in the first place.

In My Experience: It's not theory it's real, customers are king

I like to ask the question, 'Who do you think are the most important people in a good restaurant?'

If they manage to mention the manager, the chef, the waiters and the cleaners without mentioning customers this could tell a tale. You might have to give them a bit of help, but they should get what you're aiming at if they've thought about the restaurant business at all.

You shouldn't find this motivating bit of the job too difficult if you're genuinely interested in how people tick. If you do find it difficult to take an interest in your people, you might be better advised to leave it to others to get the best out of your staff, while you concentrate on the key people at the top. But that's not ideal.

Push-me-pull-you

Let's talk about your management team; let's say the manager of your second, third and fourth outlets. A good team leader has to change their style of motivating to suit the person they're working with. The main thing I've learnt about influencing and motivating people is that they're all subtly different and that you've got to fit horses to courses.

Think about your instinctive style of working with people. I naturally have a consultative style, influencing people by discussion, asking for their opinion and including them when I'm making plans. But it comes out differently for different people. For example, my influence over one key manager in my team consisted almost entirely of listening to her, as she worked out what needed to be done and how to do it. At the end of such a session she had made a good decision, knew she had my support and was well motivated to go back and get on with it.

With another person, I found I had to spell things out much more, making suggestions and giving advice. Then there was another person who was very process oriented. I motivated and influenced him by helping him through, for example, a simple planning process. He also liked to write everything down, which was good, as it saved me doing it. Incidentally, some of the processes he developed for his job were very useful in other parts of the business. I didn't hesitate to introduce them elsewhere and made sure that everyone knew from whom they originated. This is a good illustration of the fact that the best people to suggest better ways of doing things are often the people at the coalface. Get into the habit of listening hard to what they say.

In My Experience: People who play hard together work hard together

I've always believed in not stinting on parties and other activities to which you invite the staff as a group. It helps to make your company the focus of people's lives. They talk about it back at the workplace; it takes the stuffiness out of being the boss and encourages people to stay loyal to the business. One quick tip if you do it – don't drink too much yourself when you're with the group. That can lead to all sorts of problems.

The other benefit of out-of-hours contact is slightly surprising but nevertheless true. The retail business is notorious for people finding ways of pilfering from the stockroom or from the till. I've found that if people know you as a person, they're much less likely to steal from you. I suppose it's the ultimate in demonstrating that you're not a big company with pockets so deep that you don't notice or bother about a bit of 'honest shrinkage'.

A bit of theory might come in handy here. A lot depends on the circumstances of the business as well. Some people talk about 'push-and-pull' management styles. Push being the 'Do what you are told' or autocratic method; pull the consulting, more democratic way of leading people. I naturally lean towards pull, but, when the chips are down, I can switch into being more directive if events demand it. Think about how you are naturally and work on behaving differently where appropriate.

You need to encourage creativity. Sometimes, for example, it's best to hold back from influencing the team over a decision they're making. If you're too involved in getting them to do what you think is best, you run the risk of stifling their creativity. If you let them get on with it, they can come up with the most amazing insights.

What the business schools say...

In theory, you should be able to help any person who joins your operation to contribute and become a useful member of the team. If someone is performing unsatisfactorily, give them enough of your time to work out what the problem is and address it through training or, for example, experience in other organisations. If the poor performance continues, go through the process of warnings, verbal and written, still giving them the chance to improve for as long as possible. Only when that process is complete should you take the ultimate decision and ask them to leave.

But...

This is fair enough for a big corporation with an HR department and HR processes, but when you have someone who is not pulling their weight it can be extremely destructive to the rest of the team and therefore to the business. You've got to act quickly. Don't, for goodness sake, get yourself in front of an employment tribunal, but get poor performers out as quickly as possible.

If you've made a mistake in hiring the wrong person then acting quickly also means that it is less expensive to buy yourself out of the problem by offering them an unexpectedly high leaving amount. (Incidentally, if you make a leaving payment a redundancy one, you can pay it gross of tax. This sugars the pill for the person you're firing.)

From the TV Series

They don't actually pay to work here but...

When you go into the Loaf hairdressing salon, you can feel the friendly and even excited atmosphere that pervades. Richard and Craig lead the way, of course, with a readiness to laugh and joke. There's nothing heavy-handed about their management style and the customers pick up on this joviality and come back for more. It's spot on.

7 Creating brands and taking risks

To create a series of outlets you need to create a brand, with a name with which people can identify. Here's some points on branding, plus some tips on when is the best time to sell all or part of the brand you're creating.

Pick the right name

A branded outlet presents an environment where people can know what to expect. The brand represents a type and level of service that people can anticipate and rely on. Start by choosing the right name. If you choose to buy an existing outlet, perhaps not a very successful one, and stay in the same business, it's probably best to change the name immediately. If the business is reasonably successful don't change the name too quickly.

We can learn from big business here. If a major player wants to go into a new market with a new product they never assume that the brand name that works well for existing products will do just as well for the new ones. An 'upscale', to use the American term, or 'posh', to use the British, car was not on Ford's price list for many years. When they decided to sell a luxury range, they realised that the Ford name would not sell well to that market. So, instead of building their own new car, which they could certainly have done, they preferred to buy other marques, such as Jaguar and Range Rover. So, if the target market for your first outlet is similar to the existing market there may be no need to change the name immediately. Indeed that may be a mistake.

If you're growing by acquisition and buy another brand smaller than yours, be very careful again not to change the name too quickly. First of all, you need to get the local interpretation of your brand established without frightening existing customers away. Then, when you're bringing in new customers, it may be time to stamp the group's brand name on the new outlets.

The key to the right name is that it gives a clear impression of the feel of the place you're being invited to patronise, or is fairly neutral but reflects the type of people you think your outlet will attract.

There's a hairdressing chain that's been very successful called Haringtons hairdressing. The two original founders have created their dream, a chain of salons in the south of England growing now by acquisition. I love their starting point; so let's talk about that and come back to the name.

The founders, who met working locally in the Thames Valley, were trained and had worked in London. Young hairdressers with big ideas, they were convinced that bringing a taste of London to the suburbs could just catch on. 'We wanted to offer a London salon experience out of town,' comments Robert Smith of the Haringtons group. 'We had worked in London and saw a definite need locally for a salon that could offer clients the most current styles and colours, in an amazing salon environment, with caring service by professional staff.' Yep, I can see what they're trying to sell and whom they're trying to sell it to. Actually, there's a big similarity between this concept and the hairdressing salon Loaf in Sheffield.

I also like the fact that they're repeating something that's worked somewhere else. My view is that it's wrong to be too fashionable or too trendy. The market gets narrower. Don't go for the bottom of the market either, it's too price sensitive. They talk in technology terms about being leading edge rather than bleeding edge. By bleeding edge, they mean taking on the teething troubles and risks of very new technology. By this definition, ultra-trendy in retailing terms can be bleeding edge.

Haringtons believe that their success came from putting clear procedures in place from the start and devising a strong education programme. They reckoned that having skilled and happy staff was one of their main priorities, again right from the start. This is my experience too.

So, back to the name Haringtons. It's fairly neutral, but has a touch of class about it, and all their brochures and so on use the word hairdressing to explain what they do. Now, I've got to admit that I don't much like changing one letter in a name to make it somehow different. But they've just changed the normal 'Harringtons' by dropping an 'r'. It obviously works and reminds us that selecting a brand name is a very personal business.

One more quick point on names – some people believe that your business name should echo that of an existing branding or positioning. It should almost suggest that new customers have heard of you before. the Brook Gallery, a small family business in the west country, sells art. It has absolutely nothing to do with The Brook Street employment agency and is a brilliant example of this. It's not passing off, which is illegal, but making sure that the associations that people have with the name are positive and relevant. There's another hairdressing salon in Maidenhead, where Haringtons started, called Headingtons. Neat eh?

Evaluating the risk/value of a business

What the business schools say...

Branding experts talk in these or similar terms. They talk about the 'weight' of the brand, or how dominant the brand is in its market place. This is not just market share but the brand's influence and ability to survive new competition.

They talk then of the timescale of the brand. How long it has been established – the longer the better in terms of survival and growth in the brand's geographic reach.

They then look at breadth. How long is the age spread? How many types of consumer does the brand attract? How geographically spread can it become? What spread of different products or services can use the brand name?

But...

Although this looks like the sort of exercise that the marketing companies of large brands such as Gillette and Disney might spend a lot of time with, it does have some uses for the budding entrepreneur. You can look at the brands that you're competing with in those terms. How will you differentiate from the big brands, for example?

You can also use it for planning purposes asking yourself, where geographically could you expand that does not carry a huge risk? What other services might you offer from the same branded premises, and so on. In the end, it's quite useful to think from time to time in this way. It emphasises that the real return will come if your business becomes a recognised and respected brand.

It is an inescapable fact that when they set up a new business the investors are taking a considerable risk. The money spent in setting up the premises will probably represent a fair whack of the first few months' gross takings. There is no certainty that the product will sell or that it will sell in that location.

The risk then diminishes as you reach and pass the monthly break-even point on a regular basis. Then, maybe the time has come to move into the next phase of growth. This time the risk is a good bit less. It's like my experience of DIY. I don't really believe in doing it myself, because you only get to do any DIY project once. You never have a chance to learn from your inevitable mistakes and then do the job again, this time much better. That is the difference between the amateur and the professional. The professional learns from experience and repeating the same procedures time and time again.

So the risk is a good bit less with the second outlet. After the third business set-up, you've reduced the really savage risk of losing all the investors' money to virtually nothing, unless you are in the fashion business. Now think about what you've got to sell. To begin with, you had nothing but your passion and your dedication, backed up with the promise of working very hard. In such circumstances, an investor is going to ask for a reasonably big share of your business as a carrot for taking the risk. After, say, the third outlet the situation has changed. You have a track record, your skills are much sharper and you've dealt with all your weaknesses by training or by using the skills of other people. You might even have a brand. Investors are going to have to pay a lot more for your business in this more advanced state.

If the founding investors, perhaps including you, were looking for a pretty quick exit strategy for a good return on their investment, this could actually be the right time to sell some, or all, of their shares to someone paying a premium for the potential of the brand. Or they could stick around.

I raise this situation because I quite often see businesses that get to this lower risk stage of development and which then start to dream about the brand really taking off and becoming an international chain to rival the McDonald's and Starbucks of this world. They then take the business into the next phase, perhaps by diversification of the product or by venturing into another part of the country or another part of the world. In risk terms, they're about to go into another situation where they don't have that much experience and may be unaware of some of the pitfalls, or the new skills they're going to need. The risk has increased again.

My point is that, as always, it's a balance – do you want to stay in with your entire holding or reduce your overall return by taking something now and potentially losing out on further and bigger returns later on. The cardinal rule is that the value of a business is much higher when it has demonstrated success that can grow organically when it's venturing into new areas. You don't want to own a very small percentage of the shares when it really goes mad, but 'a bird in the hand', and all that might be worth having. Don't forget that you can always start over again, this time with your own money and with a nice low risk profile. In other words, you need to step back and look at the risks you are taking on a regular basis, because at times they go higher rather than lower.

In My Experience: Timing an exit

Two guys set up a publishing company with a difference. They built a massive base of intellectual property by publishing paperbacks and selling them through the book trade to consumers – a pretty standard way of operating. The brand quickly became reasonably successful, because they had the necessary skills and experience in this area.

The second part of the plan was to sell the rights to their intellectual property to other companies in tailored, paperback or electronic form. This was a venture that had been tried in a number of ways by other publishers, but not quite in this fashion, and never terribly successfully.

They've got their first two quite small corporate deals and now face a dilemma – do they sell part of the business now, with all its potential, or do they stick it out? I think they need to just go over the risk/value relationship of what they're doing. They may want to stick it out and achieve immortality with their own self-built brand or they might just want to take advantage of their profile, which is currently lower risk but high potential return.

What is the principal reason that individuals tend not to make a lot of money on the stock exchange? Is it that they buy the wrong stocks? Not necessarily; if you buy enough to make a balanced portfolio of stocks, you should do pretty much as well as the 'experts'. No, the main reason is that they don't sell at the right time. They think that a rising market will never stop. Then the crash or downturn comes and they're lucky to get out with their original stake. I have a grave suspicion that there's a lesson in there for someone building a business or a brand.

8 Get organised and look professional

Nothing happens in your own business if you don't initiate it. How well you're organised can mean the difference between success and failure. And while you're getting organised, think also about how people are going to view your business and you personally, and make sure that everything they see is professional.

As an entrepreneur you've got to keep on top of everything, 'cos there's no one else to do it

Remember the days when you worked for a big company and a light bulb went out? You might mention the fact to someone, or you might not bother. Someone else would notice it or the maintenance people would see to it in the normal course of events. Then, later on, you might spot that it's been changed; and that's it for light bulbs when you work in a big company.

In your own business, it won't get changed unless you trigger off an action to get it done, or you do it yourself. So you decide to do it yourself. The first thing to do is to get the old bulb out to see what type, make and wattage it is. In order to do that, you need a ladder, which you haven't got. So you borrow a ladder, take the bulb out, find it's a slightly unusual type and phone around lighting shops to find one; or make that two, so that when it happens again you're better prepared.

You retrieve your car from the car park and go get the bulb. The first place hasn't got one exactly the same, so you move to the next one, and so on. Back to the car park, turn electricity off, change bulb, take ladder back to where you borrowed it and guess what, it's nearly lunchtime. You make a mental note to have a spare light bulb for every type of light in the premises. I don't think that a mental note will do. Write it down. Don't forget that there's no one to tell you to do it or remind you about it. You are truly on your own.

This is not as stupid a story as it seems; you can waste so much time dealing with little niggles if you're not incredibly well organised.

I have to admit here to an addiction – an addiction to lists. Whenever I agree an action, or see something that needs to be done, I add it to my list. I carry a notebook at all times just for this purpose. Look, I don't always remember, nobody's perfect; but without my list mania I'd make a lot more mistakes. Get into the habit of making lists and scoring off items as they get done. If a number of matters have crowded in on me, all requiring quite swift attention, it actually helps to put them into a 'To do today' list before you set off on them. Once you've seen the extent of what you need to do, it can seem more manageable than if you just have all the impending events washing about in the back of your mind.

It may sound a bit odd, but I get a huge kick at the end of the day when my list of actions have all been completed and scored out. I don't go as far as a bloke I know though; when he starts his list, he puts down 'write list' as the first action. This means that the moment he's finished writing the list he can go back up to the top and score out the first item as completed.

In My Experience: Beware the cost of maintenance as well as the cost of purchase

Can I make another point using the light bulb as an example? When you're buying things for your premises, or purchasing computer hardware and software or whatever, always ask yourself and the supplier about the cost of maintenance and consumables. Some light fittings can initially look quite cheap, but can have very expensive replacement bulbs. Sometimes this is just a technical fact, and sometimes it's a marketing ploy.

I needed a fax for one of our outlets and I spotted an ad in a newspaper offering one for a good bit less than £100. I bought it, only to discover when it ran out of ink that the replacement cartridges were nearly £45. Not only that, but the original cartridge ran out after only printing a few faxes – that's the supplier's policy, sell the product cheap and then make money out of the consumables. I learnt from that always to buy replacement consumables at the same time, if you possibly can, as the equipment. And weigh up the costs of consumables in the buying decision.

You will have noticed that if you buy a computer or other electronic device in a shop, they will always try to sell you a two- or three-year maintenance service, normally at a price that is inconsistent with the value of the equipment you're purchasing. The retailer probably makes more out of the extended warranty than they do out of the margin on the equipment. I always turn them down.

Just who and what do people think they're dealing with?

In Chapter 17, we're going to look at the vital subject of first impressions – the first impression people get when they see and enter your premises for the first time. But there is another impression that other businesses, banks and suppliers, for example, get of your business, and that's from your paperwork.

At the very minimum, you need:

★ **Headed notepaper** with your VAT number at the bottom. There are some other rules about what you need to put on certain documents, so check with your accountant.

★ **Invoice forms**, also with the VAT number. Crucially, this will clearly state the payment terms. By the way, you don't have to start you invoicing at number 1. It gives a better impression and suggests that you've been in business for a while if you start with a much higher number – say 11,987.

★ **Purchase order forms**. Many small businesses don't bother with these, but I think it's a mistake for two reasons. One is that it's professional, and the other is that it allows you to record what you think you're buying, what you're paying for it and any other terms or conditions that you want to apply. The file of historical purchase orders can be useful in the future.

★ **Compliments slips**. Whenever you send back a form, a VAT return or anything else that doesn't need a covering letter it's much more professional-looking if it's accompanied by a compliments slip saying who it's for and who it's from.

In My Experience: Think of your correspondence as an 'ambassador' for your business

When I was at college, I spent a bit of time working for IBM. Of all the things they taught me, the one I've found most beneficial is how to write a decent business letter. They taught me about having lots of white space, tabulation and the importance of using simple, unpretentious English – no 'Assuring you of our best endeavours at all times', for example.

They also taught me to leave a bit of time before reading through a letter and signing it, so that I stood the greatest chance of writing clearly and accurately. If you don't have this knowledge, I think it's well worth getting it from a book or a website. You could start at: *http://www.speakspeak.com/html/d2h_resources_letter_writing _phrases.htm*

When we wanted to attract people into a club that we were just starting to get going, we used VIP passes. They were, in the end, just free entry tickets, but they had a unique number on them and we called them VIP passes. That made them look different and professional. So people kept and used them, rather than just chucking them away.

I tend not to economise in this area. By all means generate your own stationery from your computer system if it's cheaper than getting it printed, but make sure it looks really good. Use at least 100 g/m^2 paper; it's classier than lower weights. If you really take the Scrooge thing seriously, you can always use cheaper paper for internal paperwork and keep the posh stuff for external communication.

I also like to have printed labels made for sending things out. They've got the return address on them and then, if you print a smaller label for the addressee, you've got professional-looking correspondence. I also like postcards with just the name of the business or the outlet on them above a line at the top. They're great for sending a thank you note, a reminder or a quick confirmation where personal handwriting is appropriate.

In My Experience: Home-made looks, well, home-made

A small business wanted a flier to distribute in town. They designed it themselves and I'm afraid it was obvious that it had not been anywhere near a professional's hand. Unless you've got a particular talent in this area, always use an expert; it's got to be worth it in the end. Once again, fliers should give the reader the feel of the premises being advertised.

I think answering the telephone comes in to this area too. Make sure that everyone who answers the phone smiles while they're doing it. It may sound daft, but the act of smiling changes your tone of voice and sends a friendly message down the line. Answer professionally, with a statement that includes the name of the business. Say 'Good morning' or 'Hello' or whatever before you mention the name of the business. This gives the person the fraction of a second they need to tune in to your voice. They're much more likely to understand you when you say the name of the business second than if it's the first word you use.

It's well worth putting some time and energy into this area at the start of the business, so that people know that they're dealing with serious, professional businesspeople working in a friendly environment.

What the business schools say...

Any teaching or writing on telephone tactics will include good advice on, for example, being patient, making people believe you're pleased to hear from them and making sure people feel that they're dealing with a person and not just being processed. If the telephone is an important part of your business, then it's well worth investing some time in the detail of this, for instance reading Guide to Telephone Tactics, *Graham Roberts-Phelps, Thorogood, 2004.*

But...

The theorists will also tell you to make frequent use of the person's name. I agree with this, but it can be overdone. If you use my name every third word, I start to get a feeling of insincerity from you, which is not what you want.

From the TV Series

It must be a rule, because there's an exception

The owners of Loaf hairdressing are the exception that proves the rule that a well-documented plan is not optional. They do plan, but they do it down the pub. They reckon that it's so hectic at the business that for a bit of peace and quiet it's better to go off site. I call it Stella economics. Whatever they decide is, at the most, recorded on the back of a fag packet. It just shows again, you've got to find your own style. Geniuses make their own rules.

Part 2: Motivation

Have a good look at yourself before you dive into implementing your dream. Why are you doing it? Are the reasons sensible? Will they motivate you and others to go through the challenging process of setting up a successful enterprise?

A lot of people work in environments where they have little job satisfaction or are just plain unhappy. They may be bored with doing the same job for a long time. They may have become tired of the eccentricity, and occasional ludicrousness, of big companies beset with internal politics and meetings, bloody meetings. They may feel threatened by the sense that their skills are less necessary than they were to the company, and that any time now they may be invited to 'spend more time with their families'. This negative force sets them thinking about becoming their own master and telling the boss what they can do with their job.

On the positive side, they look with some envy at people who have set up their own businesses, stopped making someone else rich and started to make money the best possible way – using someone else's labour. They may have had to work hard to achieve their success and had some scares on the way, but they've made it. They report to no one, they work when they want, they make the rules and, who knows, they may even have an exit strategy by which they sell the business and end up with a whole lot more pension money than two-thirds of final salary.

Big company employees also look positively at another kind of self-employed person. These people don't seem as hassled as the first lot. They seem to have settled for a comfortable standard of living rather than risking all for luxury; but it still looks a better lifestyle than the rat race in Megacorp Inc. They work on their own, they work when they like, they dress casually, they seem to be able to fit in more golf, and they use the phrase 'seeing more of my family' very positively. They, too, have taken risks, and although their sights may be lower in business terms, they are high if you measure happiness into your quality of life. They're not trying to be Richard Branson, they've settled for a reasonable living with their preferred lifestyle.

Chapter 9 A lot of people with experience of setting up new businesses have discovered which motivations work and which could lead to trouble. Use this chapter to check that your motivation for going on your own is a positive one that will drive you to success.

Chapter 10 You're going to need help. Help from all sorts of people, but particularly from specialists and professionals. These advisers will be very important to your achieving your dream, so choose them with care.

Chapter 11 There's no point in going on your own if your work/life balance is so distorted that you're unhappier in the overall than you were working for someone else. Work out just how you want to live and spend your time.

Chapter 12 If your business depends on the British weather, you could have a rude shock. Your business plan must include making money when it's raining, as well as making money when it's fine. It can be done; but you need to make a logical and realistic plan.

OK, you know yourself well enough and your motivation for taking the risk of going out on your own is strong. Good for you; go for it.

9 Just why are you doing this?

There are some very good reasons for risking it all and doing your own thing; but there are some that are less likely to lead to success. Think hard about why you're doing it and where you're trying to go.

You've gotta really wanta do it

The first thing to say on this subject is that you are much more likely to succeed if the reasons you are leaving your current career and going it alone are positive rather than negative. Even the simple 'I just want to be rich' or 'I want to be my own boss' are better than 'I've got to get away from this horrible boss' or 'I hate this job'.

I've known people who try to build a business because their partners wanted them to do it in order to improve their status and, in the process, of course, their own. I've known people who have been so jealous of the success of others that they've set up a business to try to imitate them. Neither of these are good reasons.

Another business I knew was handed down to the next generation when the proprietor wanted to cut down the amount of time he and his wife put into it. The son left his job to continue the family firm, despite having few of the skills necessary to emulate his parents. It was always going to be a disaster, and Dad and Mum would've done better to sell it or simply retire.

From the TV Series

They just wanted a change

It's quite possible that Paul and Lee will build their café/bar in Burgess Hill into a thriving business. I was concerned with their motivations though, right from the start. When I asked them individually why they were doing it, they both cited career change as the main driving force and expanding their social circle as the second.

Passion has its place in all of this. It's good to feel driven to build a business. It's great if you get up in the morning really looking forward to what you've got to do when the project's in its early stages: it's fine to feel good about spending a lot of time in your now thriving business. It's fine, but at these two stages it's quite easy. Being positive at a time when your business is finding its feet and you know the day promises a lot of stress and problems is much more difficult. That's when you need passion and adrenalin to see you through.

From the TV Series

'Just imagine a real burger with chips that taste of potatoes'

In the first series of *Risking It All*, Naz really had a positive attitude. He had a dream of real burgers and how people would love them so much that they would abandon the junk food that, in the main, our high streets present. Naz and Mark had problems of course, but much of the reason they overcame many of them was because of this passion. They really wanted to do it.

Time to think your motivation through

No one can build a successful business without some passion and interest in what they're doing; but looked at in the cold light of day, the reasons people do it boil down to these three things: money, status/fame and lifestyle.

Money Some people simply want to be rich. They want to make a lot of money as quickly as possible and then retire early to spend more time with their grown-up families than they ever did when they were young. To do this, they have to build a dream business with apparent shareholder value that they can sell, probably in an earn-out, allowing them to do another three years in the business before retiring rich enough to do what they want long before normal retirement age.

The decisions that such people take will be as consistent as possible with the wellbeing of the business as such, but the over-riding objective is their personal wealth and they will take risks with the business in that regard.

What the business schools say...

Over-trading is a dirty word in business schools. They prefer the growth of a business to be controlled and there to be little risk that the company will run into problems with cash while it pursues its aggressive growth targets.

But...

Money-oriented entrepreneurs tend to be less risk averse. As one of them so neatly put it, 'OK, maybe we are growing a bit too fast for the theorists, but I don't want to have to dig my own swimming pool.'

Often charming, sometimes simply frightening, these people know exactly what they want and will work hard and do whatever is necessary to make that happen. Don't, incidentally, get in their way if you are a 'quiet life' person.

Their strengths include their enthusiasm and their ability to understand instantly the way they should take their business forward – their target is easy to identify. The successful ones discover new insights in how to manage a business for owner's profit, and everyone can learn from them. How much of them is in you?

Status/fame Other people want to build a business to make a name for themselves. When they make it, they will happily appear in their own advertisements and expose themselves as gurus to the broadcasters and press at any opportunity. The vastly successful of them desire a high profile, an OBE at least, and eventually seats on government agencies that pay very little or nothing but give them cocktail party access to the great and the good. They, too, will work hard and do whatever is necessary to fulfil their dream. Their strengths include their unquenchable self-belief and single-mindedness. Add to that the amount of free publicity, at first locally and then worldwide, they can generate to advance their businesses and you can see the connection between their ambition and their company's success. If they have a weakness it can be suspicion of other talented people in the business, who they fear might eclipse them. Do such thoughts lurk inside you?

Lifestyle Some people tire of the rat race and want to get out to build a more suitable lifestyle. Such an ambition is absolutely valid, but changes dramatically how they run their businesses. Their personal lives are completely entwined with their business lives, and decision making on the latter will always start from the former. Often they are fulfilling their lifelong passion or hobby, and turning it into a business that may not put them up with the mega rich, and will certainly not make them feature in the national press, but that is not how they define success.

So, just why are you doing this? Think through, and preferably write down, your objective with the new business. Make sure it's measurable. How will you know when you've reached the dream? Is the objective achievable? Yes, it probably is, as long as it's sensible. Many people have succeeded before you, and sometimes not the most likely of people. The fact is that, by following some common-sense rules and working hard and smart, you can risk it all and win.

Oh, and make sure there's a time target. You have to know when you want to get there, because we're all a long time dead.

In My Experience: Too late with the exit strategy

My business partner, Simon, believes that we got a lot right and, in the end, built a big, successful business. But he really thinks we could've done it with a bit less pain, and perhaps in a shorter time, if we had worked out our exit strategy – that is how we were going to cash in our success – at an earlier stage in the development of the plan.

10 Choose your advisers with care

You're going to need advice and feedback. Some people will do that more reliably than others. Where you need professional advice, buy it from a recommended source and pay for it properly.

Is the feedback objective?

Everyone you meet will form an opinion about your business and will, in most cases, be happy to share it with you. I've found it best to listen to my harshest critics the most attentively. If they genuinely believe that you're getting it wrong, it's wise to try to open your mind to the feedback, question any assumptions you've made and then decide whether to change anything as a result of the advice. You don't have to change anything, of course, but it's advisable to think through what they're saying. Oh, and they're often right.

Such criticism comes from all sorts of sources and you should listen to it all. 'Out of the mouths of very babes and sucklings hast thou ordained strength' – how true, oh Lord, how true. Children are brilliant sources of feedback. They tell the truth and they often represent the views of the grand majority of their peers. It is, after all, peer pressure that decides what's cool and what's not. I think I also subscribe to *in vino veritas* in this regard as well. When a person's tongue has been loosened by a couple of glasses of wine, they're more likely to tell it as they see it.

Be careful about the views of close friends and family. Their wish to encourage you, and their hopes for your success, can blinker their thinking and make their opinions too subjective to be helpful.

Using professional advisers wisely

You're going to need professional advice. This is an area where I cough up the fees. I don't, though, go for the very big national and international practices; I prefer local people with local knowledge and contacts. Used wisely, they can save you money and point you in the right direction in areas such as buying businesses and properties. Incidentally, one of the areas that I don't always use professional advice is surveying. For a princely sum of money, a surveyor will go into a property and point out the same deficiencies that you can easily spot for yourself. They'll also miss the ones that can only be discovered once you've bought the lease and lifted all the carpets. Having said that, if you're buying an expensive freehold it could pay you handsomely to bring in a professional surveyor.

Now, when I say pay the fee, that doesn't mean that you should stop wearing your bargaining hat. In Chapter 22, I talk about negotiating for everything, and this area is no exception. You've got to negotiate with your friendly professionals such as accountants and lawyers. Here is one illuminating illustration. A company was offered £1 million by a venture capital company for 33 per cent of the shares. The owners went to another company and, through competitive negotiation, got a second offer of £1 million, this time for only 20 per cent of the share capital – some difference.

Another popular way of going about buying a going concern, and one that reduces the downside risk of the thing not happening, is to negotiate what are sometimes called 'contingent fees'. You only pay if the deal comes off.

Don't, however, stint on tax advice when discussing and making bids for businesses. You can't ever know enough about tax, unless you dedicate yourself to it entirely; so buy in the expertise. They will tell you about disposals through stock dividends, things to do prior to the sale of a business, bonus dividends of shares and multiple other ways of ensuring that you do not pay more tax than your activities warrant.

It came home to me in another way the other day, when a friend of mine was talking about filing for probate for his father's estate. The estate, mainly because of the property involved, had to pay inheritance tax. This made a huge difference to the amount of time and effort required to make a settlement with the tax office. With inheritance tax at the marginal rate, 40 per cent, it's got to be well worth putting in the time.

In business it's not always clear cut whether time, the commodity you've got too little of, put into saving tax is worth the money you save. Remember that if you give the government 40 per cent of your profits, then you've kept 60 per cent. If you pay a lot of tax, it means that you've made a lot of money. You can waste a lot of time saving tax, and if you cut corners and get a full investigation started you can wave goodbye to an immense amount of your, and your accountant's, time and your money.

Some years ago, I worked in the marketing department of IBM, whose head office was in London. One of my colleagues had organised, quite legally, a payment of a bonus that reduced his tax burden by spreading the payments over two tax years. Then the administrators blew it and paid the whole lot at once. The phone lines between our office and London became hot, and the language ripe, as he tried to sort it out. He made good progress, but had not 100 per cent restored the planned position. I swear he took the next two days arguing and fighting for his rights. We calculated that the last one and a half days concerned the last and smallest item, and made a difference to him after tax of less than £10. There must have been something better he could have done with that time.

The very serious side of this is that managers can ponder a decision that makes complete sense in every way, except tax. On the other hand, wrong decisions driven by tax savings could in the end be costly.

About management consultants

An article in *The Economist* in February 1998 said it all. Entitled 'Management Consultancy; the new witch doctors', it began with the sentences, 'If you had to pick a single business or profession that typifies the frenetic second half of the 20th century, it might well be management consultancy. It has grown fast…it is easy to get into…it pays well…and, best of all, nobody can agree precisely what it is.'

There is a limited set of times when such consultants can be useful; so you've got to learn how to use them wisely. In choosing a consultant, it is first necessary to assign priorities to the skills and qualities needed.

Ask yourself:

★ What is the purpose in hiring a consultant?

★ What can an outside agency do that internal staff cannot?

Once you have selected a consultant, several safeguards must be put in place. These will ensure the smooth running of your relationship with the consultant and the most effective use of their time:

1 Have a formal contract.

2 Draw up a schedule of payment and what constitutes chargeable expenses.

3 Define the task closely and include who you talk to in the consultancy hierarchy if you have a problem.

4 Include an agreed cancellation or postponement fee in the formal contract.

I've mainly used consultants in designing fit-outs or promotional material. They can save you a lot of time in these areas and produce something that's not only professional, but much better than you could do yourself.

Bringing the concept bang up to date

The owners of Real Burger World used an adviser to help with a complete redesign. They designed new logos, changed the interior look and all of the packaging. It was a very successful relaunch and well worth the money they paid for it.

What the business schools say...

Business schools advocate using consultants in tricky areas of decisions about staffing and organisation. They believe that a third party will cut through company politics and people problems, producing the best outcome for the company, as opposed to the people in them.

But...

Sorry, but I think this is ducking the issue. Solve your people and organisational problems yourself. Be prepared to talk to people who are angry and hurt about staffing decisions that you've made without resorting to, 'Well, it was an outside agency that recommended we promote Bob rather than you.'

11 Are you working to live or living to work?

In the first days of your new business it's unlikely that you'll do anything other than solve problems and serve customers. But at some point you've got to take a step back and plan your work/life balance.

Start with a target

From the TV Series

Paul and Lee in their bar/café are just plain knackered

After six months they were talking in terms of, 'We're not afraid of hard work, but it's taken over our lives completely. We've lost weight. We're always working. We have no social or sports life. We were prepared for a change in lifestyle, but nothing like this. Anyone who thinks it's glamorous to own your own bar/restaurant business hasn't tried it yet.'

Here's a little exercise that you might find useful if you fear that you too are becoming a workaholic, either by choice or because of the state of your business.

There are 168 hours in the week, of which you spend 56 in bed. This leaves 112 for living in. Draw a three by three matrix of nine square boxes and write an activity heading in each of them. The headings will include some of the following: friends, relationships, family, alone time, health, hobbies, leisure, work and any other areas of life that you enjoy or endure. If you need more squares just add them. Don't forget to add areas where, at the moment, you do nothing, but which you wish to get involved in.

Now list the number of hours in a typical week you spend in each of these areas, convert it into a percentage of 112, and write the percentage into the appropriate box.

That's your starting point. You may wish to check what you have written with your partner and a work colleague, to make sure you are not indulging in wishful thinking. If the percentages are just what you want, well done; relax and move on to the next chapter.

Now mark the ones that are concerned with running the business and take far more time than you'd like, and decide by how much you want to reduce them. This is particularly useful if you've separated day-to-day running activities with planning the way ahead. The latter may well be an area where you'd like to increase the amount of time spent on it. Then pick the main activities that you want to spend more time on if you could get away from your business.

If you can do the next bit on your own fine, but I think this is something that you probably need to talk over with another person, your mentor, partner or whoever. There is a reason for this. You wouldn't be doing too much work if you knew right now how to change the situation. You're probably spending all your time at work because you simply have to in order for the business to survive and operate. And on your own you haven't been able to do anything about it. Another brain might come up with a suggestion, or get you to reconsider a solution that you've rejected as impractical. They might just put a completely new way of doing something on to the table. They'll certainly make you check your facts and avoid making assumptions.

It can't be true that you're working 100 hours a week because there's no alternative. Because if it were true, it means that you're on track either towards your first heart attack or throwing in the towel. The fact is that people operate more efficiently at work if they have a sensible work/life balance. You make better decisions when you have some time to think and aren't completely exhausted.

Keep asking yourself 'Why?' Why can't I leave the salon to run without me for at least a day and a half a week? Is it because the person who would have to run it while you're not there hasn't got the skills? It might be that they do actually have the skills, but that they can't exercise them because you're always there to take the decisions and the responsibility for them. In which case, can't you train them?

Sorry folks, but I'm convinced this is a very important part of becoming an entrepreneur and building a business. If you're working all the time, it means you're not delegating enough, or your systems are not clear enough for the business to more or less run itself. And frankly, if the objective is to become rich, that means you have to develop a business that still thrives when you're taking your well-earned break in the Bahamas, or living your dream of taking six months off to climb Mount Everest.

Switch off as well as on

The other side of this coin is to make sure that, when you're not actually working, you switch off completely from all thoughts about the job.

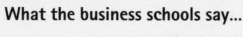

What the business schools say...

You get mixed messages from the business schools on this one. Some applaud the likes of Martin Sorrel, Chief Executive of the advertising and media giant WPP. He downloads his emails on to a gadget when he's waiting for people to clear the next green when he's playing golf. On the other hand, they proclaim that if you or your people can't do the job in eight hours a day for five days a week then either you're in the wrong job or there's something wrong with your business processes. They maintain that you can't do a difficult job well if you're having sleepless nights.

But...

My experience is that the odd sleepless night is part of the job description; but that the following day you have to do something, even something radical, to avoid another night without sleep. Take action in such circumstances and take action now.

I personally couldn't enjoy a life of emailing on the golf course!

And 'switch off' means 'switch off'. If your deputy can still get to you when you're on your day off, you haven't properly delegated decision making to them.

Sporting activities are very good for really getting away from all thoughts about work. It's quite impossible to think out a new stocking procedure if you are running around a tennis court like a blue-arsed fly, or even trying to work out how to get out of a nasty pin on your bishop when playing competitive chess. It's very interesting to note that recent research shows that exercise is part of a non-Prozac solution to stress and depression.

Weigh up the risk though. If your chosen sport is rugby or rock climbing severe-rated routes, then think through what would happen to the business if you broke a leg.

In My Experience: Try to avoid the really hard markets

The reasonably new market for male grooming products fascinates me. The market is undoubtedly there. While gay men are already quite well into moisturisers and good skin care, there is a vast market of heterosexual males out there who are targets for good marketing and presentation. I would want to go into it when I was sure that the interest was taking off and I didn't have to endure five hard years before the business started to thrive.

When you're chasing your dream, you want results reasonably quickly. Unlike a big business, you probably don't really have the time to wait around for success, and you certainly don't have the capital for a long-term bet.

It's all very well being on the leading edge; but make sure it's not the bleeding edge.

I would add one thing to this. When you go away for a length of time, say a holiday, it's easy to worry that you might be missing a real disaster while you're absent. This is why I, personally, leave the phone on when I'm on holiday. But I also ask that no one rings me unless there's a real crisis. I find it more relaxing to know there are no disasters than to sit there thinking that there could be.

In My Experience: A consultant books his holidays

A friend of mine has been a consultant for a long time. This is how he keeps his diary and puts the importance of holidays into his plan for the year:

'Very early on in my consultancy days I was with a client and took a booking to run a course. I wrote it in my diary. The same day, my partner, Penny, took a booking in the office from another client for exactly the same days. She wrote it in the desk diary that I looked at from time to time. As luck would have it, we discovered the double booking in time to avoid a difficult conversation with one of the clients, but we swore from then on to keep only one diary. Some people do this electronically, but we have stayed with the same white board above the office desk. It is slightly embarrassing, occasionally, when I am at a meeting of the board of a client and the time comes for the next appointment to be booked. They take out their personal organisers and diaries or log on, while I have to excuse myself and make a phone call. "Oh God, Ken's got to ask Penny if he is allowed to come," they say. But it's worth it for the security that we can never double book.

'When you have got your consultancy going you will get repeat bookings. Customers will ring and offer you work on such and such a day. This is why it is so important to put red-letter days when you do not want to be working into your diary at the beginning. If you don't, you will find yourself not taking a break. I start by noting the first days of the two home test matches at Lord's and the Oval. I then block out the weekends when I have to be at Murrayfield to watch Scotland humiliating various other nations at rugby. Finally, we put in the holidays. Only then do we start taking consultancy bookings.'

Apart from the rather fanciful part about Scotland winning at rugby, I think this is pretty good advice.

12 Depending on the British summer, and other myths

There is always a possibility that a change in external events will have a glorious and positive impact on your business. But base your business decisions on hard facts, rather than hopes that things will change.

Impending events

Professional salespeople have many ways of trying to 'close the business' and take an order. One of those that's often trotted out is the 'impending event' close. They will say, 'Order now, I happen to know there are only two available at this time,' or 'You would be best to go ahead now, because I hear on a very reliable grapevine that there's going to be a price increase.' Now, they're just doing their job and it doesn't matter much to them whether what they're saying is actually true or just a vague rumour. If it helps to close the business they'll use it.

During the early days of shooting *Risking It All*, I frequently heard the impending event, 'We're expecting an improvement in sales when the summer comes along.'

Looking forward to summer in Burgess Hill

Paul and Lee in their café/bar in Burgess Hill were looking forward to the summer. They had tables and chairs outside on the pavement, and were confident that, come the good weather, sales would rise above the break-even stage at which they'd arrived.

Let's look at the logic of this. Where do people go for lunch when it's hot weather? Answer, they buy a sandwich and a drink and then aim for a wide-open space like a park. They don't generally, I'm afraid, say, 'Oh, it's a scorcher, let's go and sit outside a café/bistro in the pedestrian precinct.' My feeling was that people would indeed use the table and chairs outside the café, but that it would be the same people who would have been sitting inside it in normal weather.

People who build a business plan that's dependent on good weather in Britain are taking a huge risk. It's much safer to base your plan on pretty continuous rainfall, and regard a few days of sun as a bonus. Be pleasantly surprised by good weather rather than unpleasantly shocked by drizzle.

What the business schools say...

Business schools use the example of outside concessions at big events. The question they pose is, 'You've been offered two concessions at the Queen's Jubilee procession, during which thousands of people will line the streets. You could have the ice-cream concession or the umbrella concession, and the parade takes place at the end of June.'

OK, the percentage shot is probably the ice-cream concession. As long as it's dry and at least warm people will buy a few ice creams, and if it's baking hot they'll buy a lot, an awful lot. But if it's cold, or pretty cold, and wet you'll sell almost nothing. With the umbrella concession you'll make a killing if it lashes down.

The business schools would say that both of these courses of action are too risky. The solution is to buy half the concession for both stalls, that way you're not going to make a killing, but you're not going to end up broke either. It's hedging your bets.

But...

Absolutely no 'buts' on this one. They're totally correct. Never take a major bet on the weather and try to hedge against different outcomes whenever you can.

In My Experience: The hazards of the British summer

My partner Simon and I owned a number of pubs along the seafront at Brighton. When it rained, the passing trade dropped to almost nil. When the sun shone, they came from miles around to enjoy the beach and drink some cold beers.

The difference was, to say the least of it, marked. In poor weather, the pubs on the seafront took as little as £300 in a day. On a hot day, they took as much as £15,000.

Thank goodness our business plan was not based entirely on good weather. We also had a number of pubs in the centre of the town, near the places that people visited in bad weather.

Other myths, including predictable and unpredictable events

I'm also sceptical of some other things that people say to give them heart when they're looking at poor takings. Students frequently come up in conversation. If you have outlets in a town with a big student population, it's true they will do business with you. The problem is money. Sure the bars and other retailers will take some extra money at the start of term, when the students are all flush with grants, parental allowances and student loans, but not much. Later they will drop back to normal levels. Watch out, too, for the student union facility, as it will sell cheap beer. If, for example, they expand the premises the takings of the pubs around it will be affected.

Students are useful, however, in another way. They're pretty much immune to changes in interest rates. So if you aim some of your business at students you are hedged against the worst excesses of interest rates. When you make a business plan of, say, three years, it's wise in the first place to try adding two percentage points to the rate of interest you've used and see what happens in such circumstances. But that's not the complete picture, because not only do your costs go up when rates do, your business goes down as well. When their mortgage payments go up, people compensate by spending a bit less on the luxuries of life. If the whole housing market is affected, and house prices level out or drop, then psychologically people feel poorer and pull in their spending horns.

As well as students, there's another group unaffected by interest rates and that's people with low or no borrowings. This so-called 'grey market' is without doubt a huge growth area. They've got no debt, they've got money to spend and they can spend it at off-peak times. You can factor all of these possibilities into your business plan. So if you aim right across the market of young people, old people and the huge number in the middle, you should be able to guard against interest rates mucking up your plan.

Watch out for the telly schedules. A major TV event can literally empty a chain of pubs, as I well know. February's a bad month in retail as people count the cost and pay off the credit card bills from their Christmas overspend. Students don't go out in June, because they're studying for and sitting exams. A bank holiday is a good spending weekend, but you pay the penalty the week after, as there's a backlash of keeping spending down.

Take care in London. During the summer, business drops considerably as people leave London at the weekends. The congestion charge has also dramatically changed some retail business in the centre, mostly for the bad, and there's more to come. So put that into any London-based plan.

You're not setting up your business in a cosy bubble, unaffected by national or even international events. How would the Iraq war have hit your plan? Have you taken into account any rumours of impending tax changes? And so on. You've got to apply common sense and the possibility of small and large change into your strategic thinking.

And while we're on the doom and gloom show, don't forget the fickleness of corporate behaviour. Companies can turn off spending at the click of a 'send to all' email, and they do it when they hit a glitch in their plans. If you have a heavy dependency on one large business, try to mitigate the impact of its changing its spending patterns by broadening your customer base. And keep up to date with the fortunes of your big customers so that you can see a problem coming.

Never take any customer for granted. 'Our customers are very loyal to us' is as dangerous a statement to make as any. Customers do change allegiances and suppliers, either because their current supplier hasn't kept up with the industry, or because a clever salesperson has run a cunning campaign, or simply because one of your people made a serious mistake. Companies also change, and the loyal manager who is your main contact can get moved on and replaced with another one with a different favourite supplier.

The final myth is 'It'll be alright on the night'. This myth emerges ironically, from show business, and show business is absolutely in the forefront of rehearsing and re-rehearsing until they've got it right before the night. In business terms, guard against 'It'll be alright on the night' by careful planning, research and rehearsal.

In My Experience: So you look for 'up and coming' or 'up and come'?

When you're looking for premises, it's tempting to find a cheaper area that you think is being redeveloped for whatever reason. The argument is that it's an up-and-coming area and that eventually the inhabitants will be well off, as people do up the houses and other facilities come in to meet the new needs. It's a persuasive argument, but flawed, as you're not going to make a living for the first three or four years of the business while the area improves.

Up and coming is good if you're in the property business and can wait a while for big profits, but it's better to go for up and come if you want to make profits from a retail type business in the short term.

Part 3: Skills

You'll build the skills you need to run your own business as you progress. You can't really prepare yourself for everything you're going to have to do. Unpredictability is one of the joys of creating your dream. But there are some skills whose need is common to everyone and these are, for me, the most important ones.

Obviously you're going to need the specialist skills that have led you to believe that you can do something better than other people. That's what makes your business unique. But work on these general skills as well to make sure you've got what it takes to soar.

Chapter 13 If you have a clear picture of how investors value businesses, you're in a better position to build the sort of business they want to buy, and, perhaps more importantly, choose the right moment to sell.

Chapter 14 I know I've said that everyone should work out their own way of doing and documenting a business plan, but the banks don't see it like that. They want you to fill out their forms. Learn how to do it, and learn what that document is for. There's a simple motivation for doing this well – they won't lend you the money unless you've got it right.

Chapter 15 Just because you're no longer in the midst of a large bureaucracy doesn't mean that you can ignore some of the formalities of owning a business. You're still open to being let down by suppliers, planners, builders and so on, so depend on the strength of a contract in those areas where you really need one.

Chapter 16 You need premises. You can buy them or lease them. Go through the pros and cons of both of these before you sign your money away.

Chapter 17 It's extraordinary how quickly customers make decisions on whether to go into your premises or look for somewhere else. As you plan the look and feel of your outlet take this rapid decision making very seriously indeed. First impressions are vitally important.

13 What's a business worth?

Whatever is your exit strategy, if you're trying to build a business by opening new outlets, you need to be familiar with how people value businesses. It's also an area where the small, light-on-its feet business can make mincemeat out of larger, lumbering conglomerates. Here's how to look for a bargain business to buy.

The multiple

Before you set out on the rocky road to buying and selling companies, make sure that you are thoroughly familiar with how investors value companies. This may seem unnecessary at the early stage of your dream; but if you're looking to make money quickly, understanding how a business is valued could affect your strategy for the business.

Here's the theory starting from the top. Don't let anyone tell you otherwise. The value of a company is based on the dividend stream it pays to shareholders now and in the future. This may seem strange to a small company that only uses dividends to reward the owners working there in a tax efficient way. But it's true. A company could be paying no dividends at all and still have a high value. But that value still stems from the fact that the company, or a successor company, will in the end pay out annual dividends to its shareholders. Large companies buy smaller enterprises for the contribution they can make towards profits and dividends.

Next level down: to pay a higher dividend you need higher profits and, of course, you need the cash to make the payment. If you want to sell your business, your strategy must in some way pay attention to those two requirements. Coming down to another level, investors will decide on the value of your business based on its history, and on its potential to generate profits and cash.

Potential buyers of your business or investors are, of course, aware of the profits that the company made last year. In existing listed companies the ratio that investors are interested in is called the yield, which is a comparison of the dividend paid last year to the value of a share. They then take a view on the management and their likelihood of being successful in implementing their growth plans for the future. This expectation of future dividends is encapsulated in the other interesting ratio from an investor's point of view, called the multiple. It simply records the market value of a share as a multiple of the company's earnings per share. If last year's earnings were £1 million in total and there are 1 million shares issued, then the earnings per share is £1. If the investors who are studying the likely future performance of the company are paying £20 for a share, then the price earnings (P/E) ratio, or multiple, is 20. The P/E ratio gives us the market's view of the future prospects of the company.

Everyone uses the historic earnings as the basis for the P/E because that is the only solid number that everybody has. If investors have taken an optimistic view of the likely growth prospects of the company, the P/E will be much higher than if they regard the prospects for growth as slow.

So it is with a small business. Investors will look at current profits, expectations for the future and give your business a notional multiple. The picture you try to paint of your business is one that attracts a high multiple when you're selling.

Buying a bit of a big business

The opposite goes when you're buying. It could be that your dream is based on buying out the part of the business that you work in – the management buyout. Or maybe you've got a medium-sized enterprise going and you're looking to expand by buying outlets from a big business. There are huge opportunities in this area if you understand how big companies operate.

The dream starts to loom larger quicker when you look at the process of taking over going concerns. If you have operated under the slogan KISS, (keep it simple, stupid) to build your business and have traded with suppliers and customers along the lines of, 'If you do that, I will do this', there is no reason why you cannot take this into making deals and forming bigger companies by trading businesses or divisions of businesses. It can look frightening, but it uses the same common sense and awareness that guided your approach to getting this far. So here are some thoughts about building your dream in large lumps.

First of all, if you're involved with a big organisation because you are organising a management buyout, or attempting to take over a part of their business, you must treat the people as individuals. Don't try and treat the company as a sensible or logical institution. In the end, individuals who have their own agenda for their career and reward structure take its decisions. Here's how to exploit the internal shenanigans and politics that pervade big businesses.

The profitability of an internal division is measured by the management accounting system. This has to include making a contribution to all the overheads of parts of the business above it, such as head office. It's this contribution to overheads that gives the small guy the opportunity. Given that fact, try this test. Think of the objections that a manager might come up with to your buying out a small portion of the whole business. Not the institutional ones, we've already agreed that they're irrelevant.

If your first thought was, 'Well, they'll have to find somewhere else to apportion the costs that used to be apportioned to the part of the business you are buying, or cut back on some overhead expense', you're not treating the organisation as a collection of individuals. That objection is completely logical, but may very well not cross the decision maker's mind. Think, therefore, about the decision maker. How will this deal affect his or her performance this year? Is there some way that this deal will improve his or her performance against their key indicators? It's not unknown for a deal to be struck which didn't do the selling company much good, but which enabled the managers responsible for the unit being sold to meet their profit targets for the year. That is, they were able to take into their profits all of the income stemming from the one-off phenomenon of disposing of an asset. Yes, I know its no way to run a business but that's often how it's done.

In My Experience: Heads I win, tails you lose

I know a bloke who sold his small advertising agency to one of the big international conglomerates. The deal was an earn-out based on the growth of profits over the next three years.

At the same time, the big company bought three other small agencies, and asked this bloke to run all four. He was to be paid by the division running the four companies, the impact of which was that his considerable salary was removed from the overheads of his original company. (Are you still with me?) This more or less guaranteed that his earn-out would occur at the top end of everyone's calculations; and that's what happened.

I find this story extraordinary, because no one in the big company's entire ranks of clever marketing men, smart lawyers and canny accountants saw what was happening.

Remember, also, that a lot of middle and quite senior managers have no responsibility at all for cashflow. This can be very helpful as you trade an improvement in their putative profit position (an opinion) for an improvement in your cashflow (reality). Delaying a sum of money passing from you to them may not be against their interests at all, while it may be the difference between life and death to you. Conversely, money coming in up front is worth a whole lot more to you than money arriving in a year's time, but makes precious little difference to a middle manager's ability to shine on the greasy pole.

Next, pay some attention to corporate hot buttons. At any time there are some parameters that large organisations are trying to change. When you say something to a middle manager that rings a bell with one of these parameters you have hit that manager's hot button. Concentrate your effort on acquisitions that do this. Ask yourself the question, 'What deal could I do with this person that will result in he or she getting a new feather in their cap by making a change in an area the company is focused on?'

And now, think big, unimaginably big. Let us assume for a moment that you are a small business with some substance, but still, demonstrably, a small business. Can I also assume that you are in a niche market that you understand entirely and where you have found ways of getting competitive edge and prospering? Now think about your largest competitor, the company that in the niche is the market leader, at least by volume. Now ask yourself, 'Would life be easier if these people did not exist or were on our side?' It's more likely that you could make this happen by taking that part of the business over if it's not making money, but even if it is, anything is possible.

Now look at how strategic this part of the business is to its current owners. Could it be described, even if it is profitable, as non-strategic? I know a small company that bought the division of a big company because strategically it was trying to get out of the software business. (Incidentally, the big business didn't really know if the division was making money or not.) Analyse who is in charge of the business at middle or just above management level. Could you approach them directly, or would you need an adviser to make the first move?

You will quickly see whether you can make such a business pay; then go back to finding the hot button that makes a manager want to sell no matter what the impact on the overall business is. The final point to remember is that you must think big, because there is nothing a manager in a large organisation will not do to make his or her name.

What the business schools say...

Financial accounting is concerned with the production of accounts, particularly for shareholders. The Companies Act in the UK, and its equivalent in the USA, govern the format of these accounts.

Management accounts, on the other hand, are prepared in order to assist the managers of the business. There is no standard format. Management accounts should be presented in the way that is most helpful in the particular circumstances of the company concerned. They should contain sufficient detail to permit close control of the business.

But...

Most internal management accounting systems are rubbish. There are many reasons for this, but perhaps the main one is the gulf that exists between the actual trading managers of the business and the finance departments that are supposed to present the accounts in the most helpful way. Just ask around, most managers are absolutely scornful of the management accounts. They say that they are inaccurate and useless. This can, as we've seen in this chapter, offer huge opportunities for small, lithe companies who know what they're doing.

14 Making a business plan for the bank

Whether you like it or not, you're going to have to present a case to a bank if you want to borrow money from them. Most banks ask you to fill in some standard forms. Here's what the forms include, and a few tips on presenting the best possible case.

The upside of the banking forms

Bank managers have heard it all before. Almost all businesspeople tell them that their particular business is different and that a banker shouldn't use the same parameters to judge their business as they do others. Bank managers therefore spend a lot of time convincing their new customers that, while to a certain extent it is true that all businesses do have different detailed characteristics, nevertheless no business can ignore the universal issues that any profit-making company has to take into account. No matter how difficult it is in, for example, a service company to calculate and monitor gross margin, the managers of the business must do it. There's another area where people don't accept a commercial fact on the grounds that things are different in their environment. It's the rule that everything is negotiable. No one, lawyer, accountant, financial adviser or supplier of anything works in a vacuum, therefore everything is negotiable.

All this is to defend the generalised forms that banks make their potential business borrowers fill in before they will consider their case. If the ideas in this section seem reasonable preparation work then I've made the point. I've used the headings and order of one of the major bank's start-up forms. We should take them seriously for a number of reasons:

★ You need to manage carefully your relationship with the bank, and this is their first taste of the new boy's professionalism.

★ Whatever business you are going into, the grand majority of the forms are completely relevant.

★ Filling them in ensures that you've thought through the points they ask for and then converted them into a profit-and-loss account and cashflow statement.

★ They are comprehensive. If you've filled them all in, apart from bits that genuinely do not apply to your business, then you can rest assured you have covered all the angles.

★ They are the first, and probably the last, bit of free consultancy and subsequent discussion that the bank will give you.

Now don't forget the point about negotiation. If you find it difficult to fill in one set of bank forms then you may not relish the thought of doing two. And yet, that is what you've got to do if you want to get the best deal. You need to play one off against another. If, for some reason, one turns your case down, then go to a third and try again. Perhaps that way you can still get two offers to compare after all. You may also find, if the second bank turns you down, that there's a flaw in your plan that needs to be addressed.

What the business schools say...

Presenting a good business plan to your banker is highly important. It forms part of the 'contract' between you and them. They will use it, particularly the numbers part, to monitor your progress and spot things that are slipping early on.

But...

True, but I would add a much more significant point. The objective of the business plan for the bank is to get the money. It's not necessarily everything that you have in your mind, and there may be some bits in it that you've written down to please the potential lender. It's a selling document, nothing more and nothing less. If it's convincing, you get the money, if it's not, you don't.

The forms themselves

Here are the questions you're going to have to answer:

What is your target market?

Think long and hard about who your customers will be. Paint a picture of the people themselves, and make sure you've talked to as many of that sort of person as you can. The more evidence you can give that the target market exists, the stronger this part of the plan will be. Now try and group them in some way. It may make sense to think about large and small customers, ones who will travel for your type of service and others who will only shop close to home.

Only you can organise a sensible grouping. A sandwich shop might group their customers as:

1 Regulars.

2 Passing trade.

3 Offices and shops who order in advance.

The point of this grouping is to identify later on in the process where greater opportunities lie and where better margins and profits can be found. This may mean that you'll start off looking for the business that's easiest to reach, just to get some sales. But you may decide to put the emphasis in your selling and marketing work on another market group who, once you've cracked into it, will give you better profits or larger contracts.

Even at this stage, there's a point to dreaming a bit. If you made some alterations to the product or service, could you reach another type of customer? Write the options down; once a great idea is documented it can never be lost. Remember while you're at this planning stage that dreams are about the unknown as well as the known. Indeed, it is bound to be true that following your dreams will take you in unexpected directions.

Do you really understand your customers and what they want?

Customers always trade product or service features against the price they are prepared to pay. They also look for how well your business provides customer satisfaction and what sort of relationship they can build with your people. To build long-term customer loyalty you need to understand their buying criteria – what questions will they use to compare you with your competitors? To understand this thoroughly, you have to talk to as many customers or potential customers as you can. What are they looking for? How do they make their decisions to buy?

Now you need to assess what your customers would say was their view of the ideal offering in each of the following four areas: product, process, people and price. Again, you can ask them for their opinion of what would be best for them by, for example, accosting likely people in the street with a clipboard. The points they make are their buying criteria and will fit into one of the four factors mentioned above. Customers will tell you what ideally they want from you if you ask the right questions. You may not be able to achieve the ideal the customer is searching for, but if you know what it is, you should be able to come close.

Not all the criteria will have the same importance to a customer, so the final step in this technique is to put a priority against each criterion. When you've finished defining buying criteria and the customer's ideal, think about their relative importance on a scale of 1–10. You do not want, when it comes to making decisions about what your offering is going to be, to work hard on issues that the customer thinks less significant, if it means putting less effort into issues that they believe to be vital. These priorities will therefore have an impact on product, process, people and price decisions later in the planning process. Chart the result of this work on a matrix (see facing page).

When you fill out the bank forms that cover this area of meeting customer needs and having unique competitive reasons for them to come to you rather than anywhere else, this matrix is a great demonstration of your professionalism in this key area. Tack it on at the back of the forms.

Customer value statement

Criteria group	Criteria	Customer ideal	Priority
Product or service What you supply to your customer	eg Quality or reliability	eg As good as a London restaurant	8
Process How you deal with your customer	eg Prompt service	Order taken within three minutes of going in	3
People The quality of the people who deal with the customer	eg Good product advice on matters like wine	eg Makes recommendations with a reason for the choice	5
Price The cost of the product or service to the customer	eg Competitive	eg No higher than similar local quality	7

Who are your competitors?

If you have a lot of competitors, you may have to choose a few key ones to analyse. There are many sources of competitive information. You should obtain your competitors' brochures and promotional material to understand what they believe are their strengths and how they present themselves to customers. Relevant trade journals have comparisons of products and reviews of suppliers. Your customers and prospects are a great source of competitive knowledge, as are people who join your organisation from a competitor. Now relate this information to your customer by making a chart of your competitors' ability to meet the decision criteria in your customer value matrix. You should note where they are nearer to the customer's ideal than you are.

This may not be relevant for all businesses, but it's worth a thought: most organisations see their current competitors as providers of similar products or services. In fact, this is not the case. There's often another way of doing things. If, for example, you intend to run a helicopter service carrying businesspeople out to remote islands, a current competitor may be another contractor offering to run the same route. It's possible that future competitors may be video-conferencing companies who would render the journey unnecessary. Think about what your customer requires and what other ways they could meet their needs apart from using your types of products and services. Think widely about competitive possibilities, because it's certain that there are other organisations thinking widely about their prospects in your chosen markets.

The market does not stand still and neither do your competitors. What a customer found interesting and satisfying for even a long time in the past will not last for ever. Whole organisations have, in the past, been caught out because a product feature introduced by a competitor has become desirable and even fashionable. You have to be ready for such a change, or react quickly if you did not anticipate the event. In the end, you're going to have to explain to customers and prospects why they should prefer your offering to others. So work it out now, and keep working at it until you're convinced yourself.

Who are the key people in your organisation?

If you are going to build a business you will almost certainly have to attract some key people who will help you go for the dream. Make sure you've agreed their role and their responsibilities. Check that their experience is entirely relevant to that role and examine their network. People who join you will bring their own contacts and networks that will help you in expanding sales. Write that down, along with their qualifications and skills. If you do this for everyone, including yourself, you will have a concise record of the starting point of the skills in the business. This is a good sales point for the banker, because it makes you look professional and meticulous.

Is your plan to reach your market realistic?

At some point, depending on the business you're in, you're going to have to spend money on promotions, advertising, mail shots, etc. Take fliers out to people in the street and try to discuss the business with them. Ask little groups walking past your premises to come in and look at what you're thinking of doing. Their feedback will help to answer this question convincingly.

At this planning stage, look at what your competition do in terms of advertising, and assess what it would cost to match them. Then decide whether that's a good idea in your first year before adding it to your estimated profit-and-loss account.

In My Experience: Getting in to see someone gives the best chance of making a sale

It is a good idea to be wary of the company catchall brochure. If it's relevant to your business and you use mail shots, always follow up as many of these as you can by telephone. Ask to go and see people for ten minutes to get their feedback to the mail shot itself. This approach is a good sieve. If the person agrees to see you, you're making progress, if they don't, then their 'I'll think about it', or 'Just send me the company brochure' was simply a polite way of ending the call. It is, of course, a faith position; but I don't really believe in company brochures that cover everything you do, they are no substitute for material that sells a particular item to a particular customer.

Flying Fortress

Violaine had to speak to a lot of mothers to get her first sessions filled up. To begin with, she started the conversation by explaining what the service was going to be and how it was going to grow. She got a much better hit rate when she started all the conversations by asking detailed questions about the mother's situation and requirements.

Is your price right?

You must be well aware of the profit margins available in your business. Work out a pricing policy that makes the best of this and is, at the same time, competitive. Look at how your customers expect to pay. If you're going to have account customers, what credit terms will they want? What can you offer that will be a trade-off for getting shorter payment terms than usual? Remember a start-up has the least flexibility in waiting for money to come in – they're the most strapped for cash. So, if that's your position, be innovative in looking for reasons why you should be paid early and, at best, up front.

Now look at the business process that you will need to have in place to chase your debtors and make them pay as near to the agreed date as possible. Who will do this chasing?

Who's going to do the selling and what's the bonus scheme?

Finally, think about the salespeople you're going to employ. These people are key to your early success if you need more than just you to do the selling. Even if the actual job is waiting table, the real role is selling.

I think you shouldn't, in the first place, use share options as a way of attracting and motivating salespeople unless it's absolutely necessary. It's your business, so don't give it away. If you accept this advice, you're almost certainly going to have to have some sort of bonus scheme to get the salespeople selling what you want them to. This is crucial.

The difficulty here is if you're in a business that has to negotiate discounts. If you make the bonus scheme a straight percentage of sales, you could have problems with the price at which sales are made. Most salespeople will happily accept a sale at a 10 per cent discount of, say, £90 rather than work hard for the full price of £100. Giving things away is much easier than selling them. You'll have to explain to them that giving away 10 per cent of the selling price is actually giving away 33 per cent of the profit, or even more. Work it out if you don't believe me. Here's a product with a low gross margin to illustrate the point.

	At full price	Discounted
Sale	100	100
Discount price by 10%	0	90
Cost of sale	60	60
Overheads	25	25
Profit	15	5

The selling price may only have gone down by 10 per cent, but the net profit has dropped by 66 per cent.

I have seen owners of businesses do very well by giving the salespeople incentives to achieve the gross margin – the sales price minus the cost of the product or service sold – rather than the actual sales price. That way, the motivation is to sell at list price. This may involve a more expensive sales bonus scheme, but could easily earn its costs. If there's no share option to offer the people who are responsible for growing your business then they're going to be expensive. As usual, it's a trade-off, but there is no point in being in business if you do not sell your products and services at a healthy price – so get it right.

Where are your premises?

The bank will want to know quite a lot about the terms and conditions of your premises. You need to consider the following:

★ What are the terms?

★ If it is a renewable lease, how much will it be to renew it?

★ If it is rented, when is the next rent review?

★ What are the business rates?

★ What insurance will you need?

★ How long will this space last, and would it be better to allow a bit more for expansion?

How you fit out your premises is also vital; so be prepared to explain that. Make sure that there's complete consistency between the plan for the premises and your target market. The banker will want to be in no doubt that your premises will be attractive to the type of person you described at the beginning of the process.

What are the equipment and other start-up costs?

'Premises' is a cost item that people choose because of their location, rather than anything else, and that tends to dictate the ballpark price the lessor will charge. You have much more control over the price of fitting out. The main tip here is not to get a design, and a price, to build premises that you will particularly enjoy, and by so doing pay more than is necessary. Choose a design that you think will attract your customers and then purchase it at the cheapest possible price.

Investing in the latest technology and making full use of it will probably be worth it in the end. Try doing a cost-benefit analysis on it. Look at the alternative, and try to cost that as well. If buying a piece of accounting software means that you or your spouse can do the bookkeeping, then think of the saving that will make at your accountants. The more you can do yourself in terms of printing plans in colour, doing your own copying and having your own Internet website, the more control you have and the lower your running costs. It's the fixed costs that threaten trouble when sales are poor or when you are starting up. Aim for investment now in areas that keep those running costs to a minimum.

Take into consideration:

★ How you will buy it?

★ How long will it last (remember £500 spent today on computers will almost certainly require another £500 in a year to 18 months)?

★ What are the running costs?

★ Will you need training expenses to be able to make use of it?

Finish this exercise and you have done the difficult part of the planning process. Now we have to convert these ideas and decisions into financial matrices and cashflow, a subject I shall deal with in Chapter 18.

15 Keep it simple, but keep it formal

It's easy in a small business to think that there's too much red tape involved in making proper agreements and contracts. Doing business on a handshake, however, is just too dangerous when you're at the initial, brittle stages of getting started. Run your relationships with all external parties as though you were a large company, it's much safer. After all, in the end, you're going to be a large company.

Get yourself partnership and staff agreements

The first bit of formalisation that I insist on is the agreement between the owners of the business. You can get a free draft one that, with a few changes, will probably do the job from a website such as www.ilrg.com/forms. If you need something more complicated, search for 'partnership agreements' and you will be offered forms at low cost. It saves money doing it this way, although it's one of those occasions when I think it's worthwhile getting a lawyer to go over it with the two of you.

Neither you or your business partner will probably ever refer to such an agreement once the business is going, but it's good to have it in the background. The fact you have it means that you've thought the key issues over and, if the worst comes to the worst, it spells out what happens if things go wrong.

Don't be afraid of the word 'contract' and all that it implies. If you read through a few supplier contracts you'll start to see a pattern, and you'll also realise that, in the normal course of events, there are only about four paragraphs that really matter. Pay particular attention to the paragraph on payment terms.

Right, now let's talk about staffing documentation. In big companies, most people can expect to have an appraisal system and a document with their objectives, key tasks and measures of performance. They may also have a personal development plan showing the training and other actions necessary for them to get promoted and make progress in the company. Now, I don't for a moment expect you to do all of that for your people, but they do form a useful guide as to what you need to do in relation to your staff. The delight of a small business is that you can give people feedback on their performance every day of the week if it's useful; but you should also have a regular more formal discussion with each staff member about their strengths and weaknesses.

In any case, you must give them a letter of offer covering all the usual things such as leave, sickness and so on.

You can get a full list of the contents that documents such as a draft letter of offer should contain from www.businesshr.net. Actually, this is a great site. It covers everything you need to know about personnel relationships, along with all the rules and regulations. It's like having a big company personnel department of your own, except you only pay for the bits and bobs that you want.

The key thing is really quite simple. The only way to make sure that you, and everyone you're working or dealing with, knows precisely what is expected of them is by writing it down and agreeing the document right at the start. That way, you definitely avoid unpleasant surprises and possibly avoid disputes and tribunals. (Tribunals are a nightmare, even if you're found not to have impinged on anyone's rights. They soak up management time and energy like a sponge does.

In Chapter 8 I dealt with the other documents you need to ensure that you both are and, just as importantly, look professional.

Dealing professionally with suppliers

Let's take as an example one of the more difficult suppliers you will have to deal with – the builders, shop-fitters and decorators who are responsible for getting your premises into shape in the first place. In all probability, you're going to use local people, small businesses themselves, and they're as anti-paperwork and red tape as you. But you will have to nail them down and get an agreement on exactly what work is and isn't involved in their fixed price quotation. Most people don't fall out with their builders before the project, or even during the project. They fall out with them after the project when the discussion moves on to the 'extras'. These are the additional bits of work that almost always crop up in any building project.

Sometimes the extras are fair enough. You may not discover the rotten joists until they've lifted the floorboards, and that's tough. As long as you've allowed some contingency in your budget, you should be able to cope with that. The worst extras are the ones that you thought were included but the builder says were not. It's these extras that you need to try to avoid by having a good list of works.

If the builder won't write it all down, then you'll have to do it for them. (In any event, you will have to get to a list of works in order to get more than one quotation.) Go into great detail in that list. Then, just before you sign up, go round the building with the builder confirming every item on the list. You'll be surprised at the number of other things they will come up with when faced with such a well-documented list of works.

In My Experience: Professionalism is infectious

If you are totally professional with craftsmen then you will lift their standard of professionalism. I believe, for example, in clearing my desk at the end of every day. I find that if I come in to a clutter in the morning it takes me longer to get organised and so longer to get started.

Insist on the same with the workpeople. They should clean and clear their tools, bag up any mess and leave the site nice and tidy every night. A lot of them do anyway; just make sure the others learn how you want it played.

Demonstrate your professionalism by using good building practice. Extras must be agreed as the only variations on the initial agreement that you made. Make an extras document – a list of all the extras that you or the builder have discovered or decided on. Emphasise that you will only pay for extras that you've agreed to and are on your list. It's quite a good idea, I find, to get yourself and the senior person on the building team into the habit of regularly going round the site discussing progress and talking about extras. In a big project and/or at a crucial time you might want to do this daily. In a smaller project at the end of the week may be all you need.

You don't have to be heavy-handed about this. As with most people you have to work with, it's good to have a friendly relationship with all the people on the project. The point is that you can be as friendly as you like if the work is backed up by meticulous documentation. They know it makes sense as well; if they really try to avoid such formalisation ask yourself if you're working with the right guys.

A short cut to preparing your own contracts is to start from one that a supplier asked you to sign. Read it through and you'll find it quite easy to adapt for the next situation. Keep professional though. I've actually seen people using someone else's contract and not being careful enough to change all the names!

What the business schools say...

There is a small builders contract available to anyone who wants it. This formalises the agreement of the list of works and price. You should always use one of these as a protection against a small builder letting you down.

But...

I'm not so sure about this one. Most small builders don't like them and sincerely believe that they cause more disputes than they prevent. The fact is, it is difficult to give precise estimates for building work, especially where the building is old, as they are prone to throwing up surprises.

You could find that insisting on such a contract drives away some of the builders you're talking to. They may also add a large amount of contingency money to the quotation to guard against breaching of any of the conditions in the contract.

It's your call, but I think the detailed do-it-yourself process works at least as well.

Confirm everything in writing

It's easy enough to get into the 'confirming in writing' habit. Whenever you complete a phone call or return from a meeting, just note down what was agreed and drop the other people involved a line by email or post. Then print it out and put it into a filing system that you know will allow you to find it at a later date. The few minutes of effort to do this could easily repay themselves many times over by avoiding disputes and misunderstandings.

From the TV Series

Sarah and Steve and an Italian supplier

Deciding to import the fittings for their juice bar from Italy may well have been a good idea. One thing for sure was that Sarah and Steve needed very detailed documentation as to who was responsible for what.

Importing goods from abroad has additional risks. You can only keep the manufacturer to their word if all terms and conditions are well documented. You can't so easily keep in touch with them about delivery dates if they're in a foreign country operating under different laws and business traditions.

Sarah and Steve needed to think through every action required to install and maintain the equipment and had to put it in writing before they signed up.

In My Experience: Become your own expert

Builders and contractors are used to protecting their position. When, as is inevitable, something goes wrong, they're very good at demonstrating that it wasn't their fault. Either the building itself has thrown up a wobbly, or it's down to someone else, a sub-contractor or a craftsman not in their control.

There can, of course, be a lot of contractors and sub-contractors involved, and sometimes an awful lot of people. Add to this the health and safety hazards of a major building site. Oh, and there's the fact that the building industry is notorious for companies getting into trouble, having difficulties paying their bills and going bust.

In a situation like this, the chances of everyone blaming everyone else for delays and mistakes is very high.

That's why your documentation is so important. Keep a note of every discussion and agreement. When you start out you'll find that your technical knowledge is thin compared to theirs. But if you talk to enough people about the project, you will soon be as good as, if not better than, them in your particular situation. Ask them questions about what needs to be done. Be there when they're lifting the manhole covers. Get to know your own building in as much detail as possible. When you get quotes, listen hard to the detail of what each contractor says. When you're walking round the project with the third guy to quote, you won't have any knowledge gaps to speak of. You'll be surprised how quickly you will learn and become your own expert.

16 Buy the assets or lease the assets?

You have to make an early decision on buying or leasing your premises. The argument is mainly a financial one. But make sure it's the right decision for the long term by only tying up the capital that's right for the situation.

Return on assets

A pal of mine was a consultant to a major electricity supplier in a European country. The company was owned by the state, but in line with other countries they were breaking it into pieces. The plan was, at some point, to sell the separate businesses to the private sector. During the period of breaking up the business, the managers running the company had to decide where in the new businesses the assets would lie. Take, for example, the IT assets – who would own all the computers used for electricity distribution purposes? The new IT company or the distribution company itself? My mate was absolutely amazed that both companies wanted to own the assets. There was a huge political battle with both sides pleading their case to the powers that be that these expensive assets, some really quite old as well, should be on their balance sheets.

My mate was working with the distribution company at that stage, and he pointed out that one of the key things by which the holding company was going to measure management performance was how efficiently the distribution business used its assets. And the more assets you've got, the higher return you would be required to make on them. The managers had to take another step on their learning curve towards becoming a private company. They had got used to the fact that in the public sector people tend to be judged by the size of their empire, including the size of their balance sheet. You look quite differently at these matters when you're facing competition and working hard to make real profits.

I like this story because it demonstrates why I've always shied away from buying premises. I much prefer to lease, and use any extra cash that I might have because of that decision to lease another outlet, and so on. It means that I can concentrate on return on my investment rather than working on making the assets sweat to give me a better return on assets.

If you do want to make a decision based entirely on finance, however, here's how to do it. Assume for the moment that all other things are equal; you will sell the same amount of goods from the shop however you occupy it, owner or tenant. Now make a five-year cashflow of the outgoings involved for each method. Get the insurance side right and the rates and other expenses. Now discount the cashflow for time and arrive at the net present value of the two methods and decide on the better of the two. If you don't know how to do this, get your accountant to show you and don't leave his or her office until you can do it – it's the only sensible way to measure any form of return on investment, and an absolutely essential skill for a builder of a dream business.

Remember what the premises are for

Properties and locations can have very emotional overtones. If you love a property and can envision the business of your dreams inside it, watch out that you don't lose your objectivity. In the end, the premises are only there to support your business. They're not there for you to enjoy and admire. There's more justification if you do it when you're buying a house. You fall in love with the place and your negotiating skills go out the window. You believe any old stuff the estate agent comes up with about other offers that have been made and overstretch yourself. We've all done it with our dream home; but you mustn't do it in business. After all, if all goes well, you'll be relying on managers all over the place to lease appropriate premises; you don't have to love each and every one of them.

From the TV Series

There'll be another one along in a moment

Ben and Gray fell in love with the Covent Garden premises they found. They built the whole vision of their business around the property and quite forgot that the chances were that if this property fell through, the next place they saw might be even better.

Keep being dispassionate about the premises. It's just a place to work. Properties are like buses; if you miss one there'll be another along in a minute.

What the business schools say...

They teach you that the value of assets on the balance sheet can be an intrinsic part of the value of a business. They teach accountants how to depreciate their value over time using some pretty strict rules.

But...

I don't really buy this. If you take the value of assets into account when you're buying a business you can make some pretty iffy decisions – the value of an asset can just be one person's opinion.

A way to remember that there can be a huge difference between what the figures say and what the physical reality is, is the old story of the jobbing builder who claimed to his bank manager, through his balance sheet, to have a fixed asset of a cement mixer and a stock of cement. In fact, when the bank manager visited the premises and looked around he found that the cement mixer had in it hardened concrete. While the balance sheet was accurate, the truth was that neither the fixed asset nor the cement held in stock had any value at all.

Look, I know that assets are sometimes involved in valuations, particularly if the assets are property; but it's always safer to value a business purely and simply by its ability to make profits.

17 First impressions

A customer uses their senses of sight, hearing, touch and smell to make a lightning assessment of your premises. Work hard on ensuring that the first impression is very positive. Here are some do's and don'ts.

They only do it once

The presentation of your outlet is a bit like speed dating. A customer eyes it up pretty quickly and decides whether or not they're interested in taking things further. So you need to be able to build a rapport with your customer as quickly and effectively as possible. Cliché it may be, but 'you never have a second chance to make a first impression'.

Start from the look of your place. What does it communicate to a person seeing it for the first time? Try to put yourself into your typical customer's shoes and look at the place from every angle and at different times of the day. Look at it from across the street, coming from the left, coming from the right and crossing the street to come at it full on. Listen to what it's saying to you.

First of all, there are some rules for all premises, no matter what product or service they supply.

★ Is it spotlessly clean? There is absolutely no excuse for any dust or dirt. Don't stint on cleaning – mess and dirt are probably the biggest turn-offs of the lot. Make sure everyone knows that clearing up the remains of the last customer is part of their job description. It's not just the waiters who pick up old crockery, it's everyone, chef, manager and owner. A table that hasn't been cleaned is a grave threat to first impressions, so make the time that it's in that state as short as possible. Hair on the floor in the hairdresser's, clothes still off the hangers in the clothes shop and bottles out of order in a grooming product display are all very bad news, just like crumpled jumpers on the clothes display.

★ Is it welcoming? Does it look comfortable and non-threatening? Does it look as though I will be relaxed if I go in?

From the TV Series

Avoid negative images, they're very unwelcoming

Now I know that people touching glass and porcelain objects in a shop pose difficulties. Most shop owners in such situations have had to contend with people damaging goods. But it can't be a solution to the problem to have curt instructions and unveiled threats on notices throughout the shop.

In the upmarket gift shop Reklava, the owners had so many signs saying, 'Do not touch' and 'All breakages must be paid for' that there was a threatening rather than a welcoming feel when you first went in.

★ Is the first thing a customer sees on entrance what you want them to base their first impression on? Entrance halls, even very small areas through the door, are the first signal of what to expect. I've seen such areas used for storing things or taken up by a huge untidy pile of outdoor clothes – not what you want.

★ Does the customer quickly understand the range of goods and services that you supply? By all means have some pictures or unrelated sculptures or whatever, but don't hide the fact of what you are. It can be very confusing.

★ Do the colours attract the sort of customers you want? There are masculine colours and feminine colours; there are adult colours and children's colours. If you don't know much about what colours say, ask someone who does or consult a book or a website.

What the business schools say...

'Colour Affects creates colour schemes for shop-fronts and interiors that work with the corporate signage and point-of-sale material to encourage the best psychological mode for purchase of your goods. For example, if you are selling baby clothes, or toys, everyone entering the shop is thinking in terms of infancy, parenthood and childhood – even if they themselves are grandparents. We would not suggest crude primaries, but a colour scheme that subtly reminds people of these concepts. If, on the other hand, your retail outlets are bank branches, betting shops, high-fashion stores or anything else, the colours must appeal to different parts of the customers' psyche.'

Extract from http://www.colour-affects.co.uk, *a very useful site in this regard.*

But...

Don't go mad or take risks. While there is certainly truth in the above, if you go into too much depth you could be aiming at too small a group of people. The colours have to work for the whole range of your customers. I really advocate playing a pretty middle-of-the road course, not too fashionable or trendy.

One quick point about product layout. Generally speaking, women are happy to forage through shop displays to find what they want. They don't mind browsing through a full rack of dresses to find one that they like, and they're quite happy to leave behind a trail of disturbed displays for other people to put right. Men want everything laid out in front of them. If they have to move something to see something else they probably won't, and they hate disturbing displays.

From the TV Series

Look at the premises as a whole and in the context of the location

My first meeting with Ben and Gray at their Covent Garden shop for men's grooming and treatment was very interesting in this respect. They seriously considered one shop because so many outlets in the vicinity were destination shops. A destination shop is one that people seek out and travel to rather than going to the one nearest their home or work. And many of their neighbours were male-oriented outlets.

They had a piece of luck with the next-door shop. It was a men's clothes shop aimed pretty much at the same market as Duke & Co. Its outside colours were quite neutral, which suited Ben and Gray, and they obviously took that into account when planning their own scheme.

It was in a fairly narrow London street with quite high buildings on either side. They were on the shady side of the street. People have a tendency always to walk on the sunny side of a street. This meant that most people would form the first impression, and decide whether to stop and look or go in, from the other side of the street. One argument goes, 'That means that they take in the whole premises in their first impression, rather than being close up to it, which is a good thing.' The counter to that is, 'Yes, but the look of your shop has to persuade them to cross the street.'

It's a fair debate, but given the choice I'd always go for the sunny side of the street.

And so to the people

How often have you made an initial judgement of a company or a retail outlet from what people have told you about it? The answer is probably many times. Indeed, word of mouth is the cheapest and most effective advertising and promotion you can get. But, how often have you heard someone say, 'Oh, the people are really friendly and helpful.' Probably not as often, and certainly not as often as you've heard something like, 'I couldn't believe how they treated us. They made us feel awkward because we were only having a drink.' This is not because most outlets have rude or unfriendly people. It's because nowadays you're only playing a draw with your competitors if properly trained and attentive staff are delivering a high standard of customer service.

From the TV Series

Is the first impression consistent with the brand?

Staff appearance as well as behaviour is also an important part of first impressions. In their Burgess Hill café/bar, Paul and Lee originally dressed their staff in quite smart uniforms. But, in first impression terms, they stuck out like sore thumbs. In an almost continental ambience, which is what they were aiming at, they looked more at home in a station or on a train. They soon abandoned them and went to a very casual form of dress which suited their brand and environment much better.

The people you need are bright, smiling, happy people; it's as simple as that. Look for attractive people, not necessarily in looks; but people who others want to talk to. Get them on training courses, if that's appropriate, and emphasise at all times the importance of top levels of customer service and staff attitude. Just one more point. You're not looking for brilliant talkers as much as brilliant listeners. Watch out for the very extrovert person who talks a lot without asking questions or listening to the answers – they may not be right.

From the TV Series

Just listen, always welcome feedback

It was interesting going from retail outlet to outlet during *Risking It All* and talking about the first impressions. We talked about what I understood from how the owners and their staff were presenting their premises. To be fair, it's always difficult if you've set up the place exactly in accordance with your dream and then someone comes along and says that bits of it don't work. It's human nature to respond and defend the decisions you've made. It may be human nature, but it's not the best reaction. In the end, it didn't matter a hoot what I thought of their premises; so trying to persuade me that I was wrong and they were right didn't make much sense. When customers and others give you feedback, always welcome it. Ask for further information and reflect long and hard on what they've said. You don't have to do what they suggest, but it's always worth giving it some thought, and if you're open-minded enough, you'll probably improve the next customer's first impressions if you make adjustments based on feedback.

In My Experience: A real shop for blokes

One of the best examples of giving exactly the first impression they intended was the G.Room in Carnaby Street, London. I visited this shop to bring myself up to date with what a good retailer of men's grooming products looks like nowadays. The window, which included a display around a heavy metal trunk of the sort you see in Formula One racing pits, immediately said 'blokes'. It continued to say 'blokes' at the first counter you met, which displayed a *Playboy*-style book with Marilyn Monroe on the cover and a pair of designer moccasins.

The grooming products were displayed at head height on shelves round all three walls of the shop. In addition, there was an Aladdin's cave of desirable and funky objects – everything from expensive chunky watches to false moustaches. They'd really thought about their customers and produced a masculine atmosphere that wasn't in the least intimidating or off-putting, given that male grooming products are still, for a lot of men, a bit iffy.

Add to this the very well-trained staff, who really know the grooming products, and you have a recipe for success. I would challenge most men to go in there and not buy something. In fact, it didn't surprise me to learn that the average customer spend was about £70.

You're probably going to think I bang on about training too much; but the lack of it is such a stopper to really delighting customers. It only takes one mistake or one example of bad service to lose a customer. It's not just the fact that a member of staff lacks knowledge to assist a customer, it's also that lack of knowledge of what to do or say kills their confidence. And it's a vicious circle. If they're unsure, they'll always excuse themselves to go and ask. If they do this a lot, customers become impatient. When they show their impatience, the staff's confidence continues to fall. Once an unreasonable customer has had a real go at them, you're in grave danger of their becoming difficult to train. It's also a recipe for losing them.

Your people can't have too much product knowledge or enough training in how to deal with the type of customers you're trying to attract.

From the TV Series

A great product let down by the service

At Blue Vinny, Steve and Lindsay are very knowledgeable about good food. They put an enormous amount of effort into the cuisine and its presentation. It took them a bit of time to realise that the waiters and waitresses had to back up this top quality service with well-informed conversations with customers. Unless you train staff to be able to understand your products and give good advice to customers you run the danger of letting down the product with the service.

Part 4: Money

The one common denominator of all businesses is finance. Whatever your skills as a professional in the business of your dreams, you've got to understand the basics of finance.

Ask a mathematician what two plus two equals and they'll give you an unequivocal answer – four. Ask an economist the same question and they'll say, 'Well up until now it's always been four.' Ask an accountant and they'll shut the door, close the curtains and say, 'What figure did you have in mind, sir?' Finance is an imprecise business with a very precise veneer. Learning how to talk to finance people and really understanding the financial road signs that govern your business is highly important. Get the financial plan right, and you'll fly. Get it wrong, and you're running a huge risk of failing.

Chapter 18 Profit, you'll discover, is to a large extent a matter of opinion. Cash going into and out of your business is very much a reality. Here's how to control your cashflow.

Chapter 19 All businesses start with some investment money. There are various sources of start-up finance and you need to choose the right ones for you.

Chapter 20 'Neither a borrower nor a lender be,' says Shakespeare, but for most businesspeople this just isn't possible. Think through how much you borrow and from whom you borrow it carefully.

Chapter 21   In your own business every penny you spend comes straight out of your pocket. Never spend any money unnecessarily; your own company doesn't have any money of its own – it's all yours. Remember that as you plan your budget.

Chapter 22   Business is business, and businesspeople are traders. They all make deals, so make sure you always question everyone's price to get the keenest one you can. Learn how to be a top-class negotiator. It'll save you a fortune.

Chapter 23   Is your business in a high gear, poised for the thrills and spills of high risk for the possibility of high return? Or are you cruising in low gear accepting that your progress is likely to be sedate, not too exciting, and not as profitable as it might be?

Chapter 24   If you can't see the wood for the trees, no one else will. Don't get bogged down in the detail for too long; you're there to look at the bigger picture.

Chapter 25   Don't fear the tax people. They're used to people being not only scared of them but also rude to them. Try a charm offensive instead.

Chapter 26   When you've got something wrong, change it now. Not later, not when it's had a bit more time to put itself right but has probably got worse; do it now.

Talk to accountants, listen to accountants and build your financial skills. They're vital to success in any business.

18 It's true, it doesn't grow on trees

A businessperson who doesn't understand cash will probably run out of the stuff. Always look at the implications of your plans in terms of cash coming into and going out of the business, and keep a tight control on it day to day.

So, what's the problem?

You've probably started with a fair amount of cash in the bank. You've tried really hard to keep the installation of the fittings for your business, shop, bar or whatever, inside a fairly strict budget. To that extent, you've controlled the cash pot that you started with.

But now you're trading. You find that you can get much lower prices from your suppliers if you buy in larger numbers and that they offer pretty good terms, maybe a 2.5 per cent discount if you pay your bills fast. Some of them won't give you any credit at all at such an early stage in your business; they want cash on delivery. All of them have, from time to time, been burnt by small high street businesses going bust, so they're very sensitive to your account going late; and they sure ain't going to continue delivering stock until you're back up to date. So there are huge pressures on you to pay for things early and on time.

Now look at the other side of the cash coin – your customers. OK, many pay cash and that's great. But in a lot of cases there are bigger opportunities available if you can give credit to potential customers. A sandwich shop, for example, is offered a contract to supply a local office with light lunches on a regular basis, but it's a big company and their policy is that they only pay their suppliers at their monthly cheque run. (Look, I know they could be lying through their teeth, but that's what they'll say and it's hard not to cave in if you want the business.)

Obviously the first rule of cashflow control is to pay a lot of attention to the problem, to try to get the best terms you can from your suppliers and negotiate hard with your debtors.

In My Experience: Working on the wrong problem

Under pressure, we tend to concentrate on the work concerned with meeting our customers' expectations and fulfilling our obligations – and in some ways that's good. But there's no point in ignoring significant problems because they're not concerned with customer satisfaction.

Two entrepreneurial friends of mine went into a vending machine business to meet the two owners who were rapidly descending into financial trouble. They both had their houses at stake, and they were both working every hour that God sends to fulfil the orders they'd got from their biggest customer. The trouble was that they were running out of cash. My mates had a look at the books and discovered that in March they still hadn't sent out the January invoices. Indeed, the collection of debt was massively behind.

It really wasn't difficult to sort it out; but it needed time for them to contact their debtors. Their cries, that if they spent time on that they wouldn't be able to set up all the machines they'd promised to their customer, were met by the undeniable rebuttal that if they didn't let the customer down they would go bust or at least completely lose control of their business to their creditors.

In the end, they phoned the customer and explained why there was going to be a delay. The customer made some adjustments and agreed a one-month break while they sorted out their business.

What the business schools say... Investors want profits

A big emphasis in business schools is put on understanding, estimating and controlling profits. After all, the share price of a company reflects investors' expectations of its profits.

But...

If you know your monthly break-even point (see Chapter 5) and have a good record of daily sales, it's the cashflow document you actually need to run your new business with. You can be profitable and go out of business because you run out of cash. It's very unusual for a cash-rich business to become terminally unprofitable.

Keeping your cashflow document up to date

Producing a good cashflow statement depends on four things, one of which should be easy, the second gets easier with time, the third takes up much more time than you could possibly imagine, and the fourth is a big worry. They are:

1 An accurate estimate of your fixed costs. When you did your documentation for your investors or the bank you will have filled out an expenses and wages sheet that identified your fixed costs. As you add to them, keep this number up to date. Remember, this is a cashflow, so you do not include any depreciation that comes off your monthly profit-and-loss account. If you are depreciating fixed assets, such as tills and televisions, for example, the cash implication will be under capital expenditure at the time you bought the equipment, or in fixed costs as loan repayments if that is how you financed it. Depreciation, remember, is an opinion. I'm only interested in the reality of cash. Basically, you can leave depreciation to your accountant.

2 Variable costs are those that only occur when you make products or deliver services. The cashflow will include the details of the money spent on production as it occurs. In the case of a newsagent, this is the cost of the books, newspapers and so on that they buy from their suppliers. Quite often the supplier's bill has got the retailer's 'discount' on it, so you can understand item by item what your profit margin is and plan to emphasise in your displays the products that give you the best return. Think hard about your variable costs and improve your ability to estimate them. Understand, also, the timing of payments to suppliers compared to payment from customers.

3 The third element concerns your skills in getting your bills paid. Don't underestimate how much time needs to be spent on it, and spend money on a resource to do it for you if it is taking up too much of your time. If you get your money in a few days later than is on the cashflow, you could be in trouble.

4 And finally, the big worry. The top line of a cashflow is the sales forecast, the most difficult estimate of them all. Not only do you have to guess how many units you will sell, you also have to estimate when deliveries will happen and when you'll make the sales.

Use a spreadsheet to record all of this and keep it up to date. In the early days, it's the most important business control you've got.

From the TV Series

Know what your finances are, let people know in advance about problems and you'll get through a cash problem

At the Flying Fortress Violaine ran out of cash. She couldn't pay her suppliers at the correct payment times. She phoned each of them before the bills were due and explained the problem. She told them that it would be rectified when she received a large VAT rebate, which she knew about from her cashflow document, and asked for more time to pay. And guess what – every single one of them agreed. After all, they'd rather wait and get paid later, than push the business over the edge and never get paid.

That's another thing – very often people will help small businesses if you just keep them informed.

19 Getting your start-up stake

There are various ways of getting the cash you need to fit out your new premises and get started. As always, it's crucial to think these through and understand the implications of the sources of money, as well as the availability. You've got to get to grips with a bit of theory here and make the best decision.

The theory bit – where does money come from?

To start any business you need cash up front. Before you can start trading there are bills to be paid. Your plan will have as good a budget for that as you can devise. So you start by knowing how much money you need.

The two sources of long-term finance in a business are share capital and loan capital. Share capital comes in as cash when the initial owners of the business first put their money in. The owners will probably at the outset be the founders of the business. In all the *Risking It All* businesses the owners put in a fair amount, and sometimes a large amount, of their own money. They either had it, or got it by borrowing it, normally using their houses as security.

You can find other investors. Sometimes capital comes from a private source, such as the owner's parents. Sometimes it's from the public, people like angels who get tax breaks for making small investments in new businesses. (By the way, make sure you've had a good look at this source if you're looking for external funds. The tax breaks reduce the angel's risk hugely, and multiply their returns.)

Then there are venture capital funds, professional investors who build a fund using money from many personal and institutional sources and invest it in a portfolio of start-up and emerging businesses. This has the effect of spreading investors' risk. Mind you, the success rate with venture-capital-funded businesses is not high. The fund managers only expect one or two in every ten to really fly. But they expect to make a princely return on the few that make it.

Then there are softer touches, sorry for the pun. The Prince's Trust helps young people to get started, not only with finance, low interest loans and small grants for market research, but also with advice and help from experienced businesspeople who put their time in for free. You can find details at www.Princestrust.org.uk.

The implications of the two types of capital are different. In one sense, share capital is cheaper. In the long run, return on the shareholders' capital comes in the shape of dividends that are normally paid out by the company twice a year. But in the early stages of a business the owners may very well drop the requirement for dividends and allow the managers to keep all the profits in the business for expansion. At that stage, the money could be said to be free.

There is also no necessity for the managers to plan to have the cash to buy the shares back. In practical terms, the money is in the company for ever. There is a cost downside in using external share capital to get a business going; lawyers and accountants don't come cheap, and you can't avoid them. Oh, and you have to find someone who's happy to take the pretty big risk of putting money into a business which may very well fail, with the consequent loss of their entire capital injection. It's this risk of failure which makes shareholders demand, in the long term, that their overall returns should be higher than the providers of loans. They get this return through the growth of cash dividends, which they can take over the long term. Or they look for growth in the capital value of the business and therefore their shares. The capital value of a business is what someone will offer for it and then pay. Venture capitalists want out. That's what they're for – a quick high risk with a fairly short term and large return.

Loan capital is probably cheaper to arrange. It comes from banks and financial institutions that measure the risk of the company and then charge an interest rate to reflect that risk.

There is a huge irony here. Time out for a moment to make sure you understand where financial lenders are coming from. If someone offered to lend you £10 for a week, but asked you to agree to pay back twice that amount at the end of the loan period, you wouldn't need to have read this book to realise that that's a very bad deal. Suppose, however, that you are completely broke and know that you will have £121 in cash by the day at which you have to make the capital and 100 per cent interest repayment – still not interested? Ah, I forgot to mention that your two children haven't eaten properly for 36 hours and that they're wailing for food. In such circumstances, the loan sharks of the inner city sink estates make such loans, and prosper. This is a good starting point for considering the purveyors of loan capital. They're all like that, only some are better dressed and less physically threatening.

Their view is that they tailor their interest charges to protect themselves against the risk of default. The more difficult the situation the borrower is in, the higher the risk and therefore the higher the price of help.

If you are running a huge conglomerate and wish to borrow $250 million to buy up a subsidiary in another country, you will be wined and dined by various moneylenders eager to get your business at, perhaps, less than 1 per cent above the rate at which the banks themselves borrow money. If you need £20,000 to tide your corner shop over a refurbishment, you will probably have to trawl the high street to find a lender willing to lend you the money at 5 or 6 per cent above the base rate. And they will probably want you to back the security of the loan by remortgaging your house or leaving your kids with them as hostages. (I made that last bit up.) Banks are indeed the people who lend umbrellas to small businesses only when it isn't raining.

Don't forget that with loan capital you also have to plan the repayments to keep within the agreed contract when the loan was made. Another irony here. If you have loan capital in your business, and even if you're making a reasonable profit, you can still get into trouble when the time comes to find the cash to repay the loan. This is one more reason for the absolute critical issue of developing a cashflow document and keeping it scrupulously up to date. See Chapter 18 – It's true it doesn't grow on trees.

One last thing on the theory – a lot of budding entrepreneurs think they have to know about the bookkeeping and accountancy side of the business, and in some ways it may be helpful to do so. But actually you can get people to do this for you for relatively small amounts of money. The topic of loans and capital is actually much more important if you are trying to make serious money. You've got to understand return on investment. It's what it's all about. You're putting your own money in and, however you make it happen, the aim is to get the fastest and largest return on that cash that you possibly can. Keep that in the front of your mind when you're making decisions.

If you're light on knowledge in this area it will pay you to read up on it a bit. There's a very practical book on the topic *Smart Finance* by Ken Langdon and Alan Bonham, Capstone, second edition, 2004.

In My Experience: Banks and borrowing

Look, I suppose I've got to be fair to bankers. I mean, why should they lend you money when you have no track record of running a business? You have to earn the right to have a bank as an interested business partner or money supplier.

Talk to them about how to do that. Ask them to paint a picture of what your business would have to look like if they are to help with the next phase of expansion. If you're talking to a banker who has worked with a lot of small businesses, their experience could be very useful.

Right, back to the practicalities of all this

I am the living proof that you can actually start a business using credit from a number of credit cards. I had enough money to buy the lease of a bar and pay the first month's rent. I needed £21,000 to fit it out, decorate it and buy stock. I maxed four credit cards and got the £21K. OK, I know it's expensive if you keep a credit card loan for a long period of time, but in the short term it's ideal. You've already earned the credit rating from the card providers, so you don't even have to tell them what you're doing. And you don't have to pay much of it back each month. Not only that, but you can get discount interest rates when you first take the card and then at the end of the discount period change the loan to another provider. It's quite possible; you just have to be organised enough not to make a mistake in your timing.

I worked out that if the cashflow I had planned for happened I could juggle the credit cards for a while and then get them paid off in a sensible amount of time. Oh, and I didn't want to spend the time and energy persuading someone else to lend the money to me, when it was already available at the swipe of a card.

Where else can you look? We've talked about remortgaging and it's difficult to avoid this if you've an asset – the house – but no business as yet. So you may have to do it. Finally, shareholders don't give money to everyone, you know. They look for the smart folk. I've done it myself. I very much enjoyed helping a mate to set up a food franchise in pubs.

One final point on borrowing. If you're leaving a reasonably well-paid job to go on your own, borrow the money before you leave, using the creditworthiness earned by your regular income. Don't tell the lender you're going to give up work and take a huge punt; you'll only make them nervous, which doesn't matter, but you'll stop them lending you the money as well, which does.

What the business schools say...

To attract share capital into a new business, the board needs a credible business plan that promises a return commensurate with the risk of failure. It should cover three years in detail and years four and five in outline.

But...

I personally find three years a bit long, but OK provided you keep going back to it and revising it in the light of actual performance. I tend not to give much away in my long-term plan, so years four and five look pretty much like a continuation of the previous year with 10 per cent added everywhere. It saves time, and it's probably as accurate as trying to work out what will really happen.

From the TV Series

Leaning on friends

Richard and Craig at Loaf the hairdressers in Sheffield wanted to make their salon look really cool and modern. Leafing through magazines, they found exactly what they wanted. They'd chosen Italian design furniture and mirrors, in chrome and steel. They were very beautiful, just what they wanted, but very expensive. Some of the mirrors, for example, were a snip at £4,000 each.

It was time to call in some favours. They leant heavily on their friends in the steel industry, for which Sheffield is justifiably famous, showed them the magazine and got the same style made up for them at a fraction of the price. The same mirror now came in at £200.

Two clues here. You don't have to have the designer label to get the designer quality, and look after your mates and everyone else at all times. You never know when the opportunity will come up for them to repay the little things you did for them.

20 The ups and downs of borrowing

To borrow or not to borrow, that is a tricky question. On the one hand, borrowing helps you to grow your business much faster than sticking to your own money, and can hugely increase your return on investment. On the other hand, if the business doesn't fly, you're not back to square one, you're back to minus a huge sum or even your house.

The benefits of borrowing

Some people believe that you shouldn't borrow at all to set up and grow a business. They advocate growing only as fast as the money you're making in the business will allow. This is good practice, and has one very good side effect – it means that you don't remove cash from the business early on, because you have to leave it there to finance another outlet or a refurbishment, or whatever.

> ### In My Experience: Don't mistake turnover for disposable income
>
> When the money starts to come in to your dream company, it's very easy to get carried away. Businesses can become cash rich at times,

even when they're not really producing the profits for the owners to take out and spend.

Simon and I couldn't quite believe it when the first two bars really started to bring in customers who were spending much more than we had expected. After all the hardships, particularly living on very little money personally, it was a huge relief. It went to our heads and we spent it.

We went out and bought cars and houses on a wave of optimism – and guess what, we were in administration a further six months down the line.

The lesson is: it's not how much you're taking, but how much you're making. Don't take cash out of the business unless it's demonstrably making profits.

Now let's look at the upside of borrowing, or 'gearing'. Gearing is the ratio between the amount of money the owners have put into the business compared to the amount they've borrowed. The higher the borrowing, the higher the gearing or leverage, and the more exciting the ride.

Most people have at least one 'leveraged play' in their financial life. They buy a house using a little of their own money and a lot of the building society's. If the asset increases in value, as it always has done over the long term, then the profits gained go to the borrower, who only has to carry out the obligation to the building society of paying the interest and repaying the capital. This can have an extraordinary impact on your finances. Suppose you buy a house for £100,000 using £10,000 of your own money and borrowing £90,000. Twenty-five years later, even if you have not paid off the loan, the asset has become worth, say, £250,000. This £160,000 is all yours, giving an average yearly return on your original £10,000 investment of £6,400, or more than 60 per cent per annum. It is almost impossible, except with a really long odds bet like the lottery, to do better than that. (Incidentally, if a finance person says that I should reduce the return by the cost of the loan interest, I reply that you had to live somewhere and the interest was the cost of having somewhere to live.)

The point is that you are making a return on someone else's money. So it is in business. If you put in £10,000 and a bank puts in £90,000 to buy a business valued at £100,000, then, if you double the profits and therefore the value of the business, you get the return of £100,000 for your initial outlay of £10,000. If you have doubled the profits in a year or two, that return is pretty good.

This is, of course, another reason for not giving ownership of the business away in share options when the value is low. This is called 'financial leverage'. Its cousin, 'operating leverage', is covered in Chapter 23.

What the business schools say...

I've actually heard a senior lecturer in a business school, not mine I'm glad to say, instructing businesspeople that they should always aim to have two pounds of their own money in a business, even a new one, for every one pound they borrow.

But...

I mean, what's he on? If we kept to that rule the economy would grind to a halt. I've never found such a rule of thumb. If you can take £100,000 of your own money and £1 million of the bank's and make a profitable business you get a cracking return on your investment – just ask Malcolm Glazer, the current owner of Manchester United.

And now the downside

The buzz of high gearing is great when things go well. The excitement palls a bit if things go wrong.

Take the same example. If you put in £10,000 and a bank puts in £90,000 to buy a business valued at £100,000, then, if things go wrong and the profits halve, the value of the business is now £50,000. Then the bank gets cold feet and calls in the loan. You still owe them £90,000 and, of course, you'd planned to pay the interest from the original level of profit. You've levered yourself into deep poo.

It's also easy to get someone excited about your idea but lose it all by not considering what happens if not everything goes according to plan. Before you borrow money, think hard about all the implications. Take interest rates. In my business lifetime the bank rate has been as high as 15 per cent and as low as $3\frac{1}{4}$ per cent. Even though it's been stable for a while now, you never know. Have a look at the business plan and try the numbers again with interest rates double your original estimate. It could make you reconsider some parts of the plan.

Look around you and remember that interest is a heavy cost on your business. Are you explioting the full potential of all your assets? I found, for example, when I had to pay £200 a month in interest for a loan, I could let out a room in my house for the same amount. That made me much more comfortable. OK, I had the slight inconvenience of someone else living in my house, but I also had the satisfaction of knowing that the interest payments were covered.

In My Experience: Just because it's in the budget doesn't mean you've got to spend it

I find it odd, sometimes, that people take a different view of money when it belongs to a company. This is true even if it's their own money in their own company. Take, for example, setting budgets for a big project such as a refurbishment of an outlet. I've never seen anyone underspend in such circumstances. I've often seen people having to add a bit more money to make it work, and that's fair enough. But why do they never find a cheaper way to do something halfway through the project? This is true even if it's their own money in their own company.

It's a mystery, but I think the explanation is that it doesn't seem like real money when it's in the business and in the budget. The lesson is clear. Just because it's in a budget doesn't mean you have to spend it. Never stop looking for ways to do things at less cost.

In My Experience: A whip-round can cause a backlash

Losing a bank's money is painful enough. It's even worse if the money you've lost is not yours but belonged to your family and friends. It's a nice idea, everyone you know putting in a small sum to get you

started. But think ahead to what it will be like if the business doesn't fly and they lose the lot. This may make you take less from some people and none from others. It's bad enough losing money; it's worse if you lose your friends at the same time.

'Neither a borrower, nor a lender be;
For loan oft loses both itself and friend.'

Quite so, Mr Shakespeare.

21 Make Scrooge look like a big spender

Spending money is a lot easier than making it. There's a simple financial rule that tells you why you should look at every element of finance and try to improve it.

Big companies have a bigger problem in this respect

It is often the cry from top management in big organisations that their people should spend the company's money as though it were their own. The chairman of a very successful, Top 100 company in the USA continually wrote about this in his statement in the company's annual report. The first year he talked about the need to reduce operating expenses. The following year he used quite intemperate language to say that he was sick and tired of demanding that managers curtail their expenditure. It was only in the next year, some three years after the need first became urgent, that he congratulated people on having changed the ratio of expenses to sales. If it takes a company of this size and quality that length of time and that type of public statement to make it happen, it is plainly a problem.

In My Experience: Actually working for Scrooge

At the beginning of my career, I worked for a man who was known as the meanest man in the bar trade. He insisted on signing off any expenditure of more than £5. For a long time after I'd left the company, I still got little tremors when the phone rang, wondering if he was about to blast me for some small expenditure I might have made. But he taught me a lot. He definitely got his company culture very averse to spending money.

Of course, you don't have the problem of spending frugally by *pretending* that the money is your own, because quite simply it *is* your own. And even when you've got money in the bank, in fact especially so then, you have to continue to bear down on costs.

From the TV Series

Should they go Italian?

Sarah and Steve were planning the fitting out of their new health food café Sejuice. They had a great location in a trendy area of Brighton with a big footfall of passing trade. Is trendy the right word? Well, Bohemian might be better. The shops around had a used, rustic look and the passing trade was essentially young, student-like and, yes, trendy.

They fell in love with some Italian-made shop fittings – counter, fridge and freezer equipment. There's no doubt it looked good. It was stainless steel, ultra modern and allowed people to drink their smoothies while standing at the counter. It also had that indefinable Italian touch to it, difficult to describe, but classy.

Off they went to the factory in Italy, and decided to spend £25,000 on this gleaming, and admittedly beautiful, kitchenware. I had two questions to ask. The first was to probe into whether the stuff looked too grand for the area their shop was in; but that's the subject of Chapter 17. The second question was about the cost of the equipment and the risk of buying from abroad.

Take it from me. A local shop-fitter could fit out a juice bar in wood or MDF and provide the necessary fridges and freezers for about £10,000.

Now, when you're taking the risk of starting a new business, it makes good sense to keep the capital expenditure as low as you can. No matter how well you've researched your products and market there's always a risk that you won't, at least initially, reach the sales figures you want. So limiting your risk by spending money as frugally as you can makes huge sense.

It could be that the appearance and 'wow' factor of the Italian equipment might do the trick and pay for itself in added custom, but it's hard to be sure at this point. And remember, importing goods from abroad has additional risks. It's difficult to keep on top of the manufacturer to make sure they deliver on time. Who's insuring it while it's in transit and how will you maintain it in this country? The most beautiful fridge in the world is worse than useless if it can't keep things cold until a spare part arrives from Italy.

Look after the pennies...

In My Experience: Make a budget and stick with it

Here's an example of a budget going wrong. The original budget for a refit of new premises was £500,000. The owners knew the concept of what they wanted and it was, to say the least of it, classy. They were going to attract well-off commuters in an up-and-coming part of London who would pay a premium to use their sports and other trendy facilities.

Their builders liked the project too; it was unusual and the customer was obviously interested in doing things properly. They talked them in to adding extras from time to time. It's the old, 'Well, you know, teak would look so much better than pine in this part of the superstructure; and it's the ideal wood for this application, very durable. It'll last for ever.'

The result was that they blew the original budget up to £900,000. Now, however they raised that money they've got a huge increase in their outflow of cash, and probably a similar reduction in what they make out of the business when they sell it. They're either spending money annually on interest charges, or they've got to pay back the money they've borrowed from friends and family, while they're running the business or when they sell it.

Again, Dickens said it first, not this time in the guise of Scrooge, but using the voice of Mr Micawber in *David Copperfield* – 'Annual income twenty pounds, annual expenditure nineteen six, result happiness. Annual income twenty pounds, annual expenditure twenty pound ought and six, result misery.'

Here's a way of thinking about margins – the difference between what you make and what you spend. I heard it from a managing director. I can honestly say that I was completely gobsmacked with the simple logic, and it has heavily influenced how I have run my businesses ever since. It's a model that I think any entrepreneur would be wise to have engraved on their minds.

Take a profit-and-loss account, projected or historic, and adjust all the main subtotals by just 2 per cent. Here's an example. This is your current plan for your business:

	No. of units	Price per unit	Total
Sales	100	10	1,000
Variable costs	100	6	600
Fixed costs			300
Profit			100

From that plan you find one or two problems. The customer has a cheaper offer from a competitor. It's not much cheaper and if you could knock just 2 per cent off the price per unit you can meet that challenge. There's also a general downturn in the high street and the number of units you're selling is going down by just a little bit – 2 per cent.

Your main supplier has announced an increase in the price of the product; it's only 2 per cent, but in the competitive circumstances you can't pass this on to the customer. Oh, and you've given your full-time staff a small increase at the half year. The business is doing quite well and you wanted to make sure that your people are highly motivated to keep it up. It's not a major increase, but it's added 2 per cent to your overheads.

You know that these four changes to the plan are all against the interests of your profit-and-loss account, but the numbers seem small, customers have a lot of choice, and it feels right to make these small changes.

Look at the actual damage this decision makes to the profit-and-loss account:

	No. of units	Price per unit	Total
Sales	98	9.8	960.4
Variable costs	98	6.12	599.76
Fixed costs			306
Profit			54.64

Each 2 per cent adjustment, all to your disadvantage, has combined to knock nearly 46 per cent off your profit.

Try out this positive use of the rule. Have a look at your projected profit-and-loss account or cashflow document and apply the rule of 2 per cent positively. What would happen if you added 2 per cent to all your prices and encouraged the counter staff to increase each customer's spend by asking them if they wanted something else – cross-selling. Perhaps overall they could increase customer spend by just 2 per cent. Now talk to your main suppliers and find a way of getting an additional discount of 2 per cent. That leaves the overheads. Go on, there must be some way you could shave 2 per cent off the fixed costs.

Interestingly enough, if you make the figures go the other way, you get a similarly dramatic impact:

	No. of units	Price per unit	Total
Sales	102	10.2	1,040.4
Variable costs	102	5.88	599.76
Fixed costs			294
Profit			146.64

Make it happen and, like Mr Micawber, get the result – happiness.

In My Experience: Make sure you're always up to date with competitive prices and activity

Keep a constant watch on what your competitors are doing. I used to check on the prices being charged by the other bars in the area on a weekly basis. With some of the competitors we actually agreed to let each other know what we were doing on pricing. It wasn't a cosy way of agreeing prices – it was an aggressive, competitive market – but just a recognition that we were going to trog round each other's bars or get someone else to do it, so we might as well be open with each other.

However you organise it, this information is vital to your being able to set your prices in the exact area of the market you have chosen.

Things never stay the same in business for any length of time

On one occasion when I went to see the Blue Vinny restaurant, I noticed on my way that the pub across the road was advertising a new chef with a qualification and a good reputation. They were also advertising a three-course meal for £17.50. This happened to be the same price as the average price of a Blue Vinny main course.

I asked Steve and Lindsay what they thought about this and found out that it was news to them. You've just got to be very observant and realise that everything changes all the time. You can only position yourself in the market if you are up to date and understand it.

22 Negotiate for everything

You've got to get the right attitude to your suppliers. It doesn't matter whether they're a big company or a small one, a builder doing a one-off project or a potential long-term supplier, you must always negotiate for absolutely everything.

Business is all about doing deals

The starting point of many salespeople, particularly big company reps, is that there is no room for negotiation. They have a price list, plus a set of criteria to identify what type of customer you are, which determines the price they must charge you. Good try, squire, but it's just not true.

In My Experience: Negotiate strongly and often

The brewers, particularly the big ones, didn't like it, but we used to re-negotiate all our prices with drink and food suppliers on a strict six-month cycle. A straightforward whinge about profit margin problems is not the best way of going about this. You need to prepare carefully.

We would give them good reasons why they should vary their price: competitive pricing in the area, a rise in the volume we were selling, an offer to display their product more prominently in exchange for a lower price, indeed anything with some business sense behind it. We knew we had to give a reason because if we forced a straight reduction in price from a rep we knew it would cause them a problem if they had to defend the extra discount with their boss. If we gave them a reason for the discount that at least showed the semblance of a win/win negotiation, and meant they could get the price change through much more easily. (Also, we found, if you just screw someone into doing something they really don't want to do, they often harbour resentment and a desire to get back at you some time in the future.)

We tried never to go down the one-supplier route. We always found alternative suppliers or alternative products, and always made sure that everyone knew we were shopping around. Plus we had no compunction in changing suppliers if we found a better deal. As the Australians say, 'Business is business, and love is bullshit.'

Don't forget the huge importance of all this. The bigger the margin on the direct cost of your product or service, the quicker you get to break-even. And once you've got to break-even, the margin on the next product you sell is all yours as profit. You can spend it or re-invest it for growth.

I'm quite fascinated by negotiating techniques. Looking around, I think a lot of successful businesspeople and negotiators use a friendly and affable manner to their suppliers, while at the same time being quite happy to be as hard as nails if it's good for their business.

I like to form relationships with salespeople because when it comes to the crunch it often means that I can get a better deal. But they're clever, these salespeople, and if they're good at their jobs they can use that same relationship to lock you in and give you worse than their best price. Watch, also, for how they use a keen price to get your custom for the first time and then slowly ratchet it up as time goes on.

What the business schools say... selling is about relationships

In the business schools they spend a lot of time talking about selling and marketing techniques. They teach students processes such as account management and sales planning that are aimed at getting the most profit out of a customer on a regular, and virtually competition free, basis. They explain how hospitality events and entertainment are good investments to lock customers in. After all, who wants to change suppliers if it means giving up the day at Doncaster Races or the ticket to a Test match?

But...

You've got to think about this the other way round. When you're getting started, the reps you're meeting are better trained at selling than you are at buying. Make sure you're not sucked into a relationship that lowers your ability to get the best deal. By all means, keep salespeople close physically in terms of talking about your business and even having fun, but keep your distance mentally. Don't drop your guard or settle for a worse deal than you could get elsewhere because you know the rep is relying on your business to pay for the family holiday. (Yes, they'll tell you loads of things like that – these guys really are only after one thing.)

A quick guide to negotiating

While your own negotiating method will become very personal, and you'll get better at it with practice, it's worth looking at a bit of negotiating theory as a basis to build on.

Negotiating is a part of our lives, we do it all the time. In fact, we do it so often we probably don't always realise that we're doing it. If you have children, you've probably already done some negotiation today at the breakfast table. Imagine telling a child that anything at all is non-negotiable. Fat chance. You can learn a lot from watching children negotiate. They have no inhibitions. They are prepared to use the sanctions they have available to them and they are completely devoted to the present, with no thought for the future. These are all negotiating skills we lose as we grow up.

The first rule of negotiation is preparation. Do not go into any negotiation to 'see what they are going to say'. Prepare positively. Look for reasons why the other person should see that your custom is valuable. The second point about negotiating is that preparation includes knowing exactly what your objectives are. Look for objectives beyond, for example, price. Could they pay for some promotional material? Could they throw in some training for your people? Think widely. What else could you get from the other party? Now put those objectives into priorities. You will have some objectives that you must achieve, some that you are going to work hard to achieve and some that would be nice to achieve. Now think of the other person's priorities in the same way. In fact, think about all aspects of the person with whom you are about to negotiate. The more you understand them, the more likely you are to find a solution they will deem acceptable.

Now you get into the discussion stage. The key to doing well at this stage is to listen. Look at it this way. If you listen more than you talk in a negotiation it almost certainly means that you know more about the other party than they know about you. Find out as much as you can about their bonus schemes, their targets, their company's year-end and so on. (This last one is very important. Most reps are under some pressure at the end of their company's month, quarter and year. They're vulnerable, and likely to discount at such times because they may need your order to make their monthly, quarterly or annual target.) This logically leads you to understand an outcome that you know suits them. You already know the outcome that suits you, that's why you worked out your objectives.

The opposite of listening in negotiating is interrupting. When you interrupt someone you are telling them to shut up. You are demeaning their arguments and suggesting that they cannot say anything useful to take the matter forward. If you imagine telling someone to shut up, instead of just interrupting, you can see that they would soon have the negotiation at loggerheads. Try to listen until they've finished speaking.

Listening hard logically leads you to understand what negotiated result suits them. You already know the result that suits you, because you have worked out your objectives. You're then in as good a position as you can be to suggest a deal.

When it comes to making bids or proposals, always start very high or very low. If you're buying, go lower than you think you could possibly get away with, and if you're selling go just as high. There's some good research on this that says that the higher or lower you start, the higher or lower will be the outcome. If, for example, a decorator normally works for between £12 and £16 an hour and you start the bidding at £12, you're very likely to end up at £14. If, on the other hand, you offer £10, you're more likely to end up at £12 or £13.

It's quite a good idea when negotiating to have some concessions ready. If you know, for example, that providing the builder's skip was not mentioned in the fixed price quotation and that you may have to pay for it, then make the point that they should have to provide it. Then later on, very reluctantly, make a concession and agree to pay for the skip if they will concede something else.

Concede as though they were drawing teeth – it gives the appearance that you're stretching yourself to your limit. The other side of this is that whenever a negotiator makes a quick concession, always assume that you can get more out of them.

Finally, make sure that you summarise all the points that have been agreed and then write a confirming letter.

The profit/value balance

At Blue Vinny, Steve was struggling with his profit margin. We had a chat and talked about the three things he could do to improve matters:

★ He could put his prices up.

★ He could make the portions a bit smaller.

★ He could pay less for his raw materials.

Some time later, he revealed that what he had done was simply to put his prices up without making any alterations to the two components of costs. He didn't want to make the portions smaller because he felt they were the right size, and he didn't want to look outside his current suppliers of ingredients because he had a good relationship with the salesperson.

I worried about this, because the price/value/quality relationship was getting out of balance. And not changing a supplier because of your relationship with a salesperson can't be good business practice.

From the TV Series

Playing both ends off against the middle

At Loaf, Craig is a naturally talented negotiator who doesn't stop short of any tactic to get the best deal. Because the hairdressing salon was quite high profile in Sheffield suppliers of grooming products were keen to have their products on their shelves. Craig would listen to the best deal that supplier 1 offered and immediately phone supplier 2, tell them the deal he'd been offered and invite them to beat it.

They frequently did, and Loaf have ended up with some ridiculously good bargains.

23 Gearing

Once you've covered the fixed costs in your business, profits take a dramatic turn for the better. This concept of operating leverage will teach you a lot about how to run your business.

Making money at the margin

At break-even point, the sales revenues have paid for the variable costs of the products and the fixed costs of the business. This means that every penny of the contribution comes through to your net profits. There are only the direct or variable costs of the product or service you're supplying to take off the price the customer paid, the rest of it's yours.

There's a huge benefit to be gained if a company can increase its sales volumes without increasing its fixed costs. It illustrates what managers mean when they talk about 'having to sweat the assets'. When you have spent money on infrastructure of any sort, slight increases in sales have an unexpectedly high impact on the bottom line. The concept of operating leverage shows the benefit of this.

Look at the impact on the bottom line of different splits between variable and fixed costs. Each of the four profit-and-loss accounts is built to answer the same question. 'If we can increase sales volume by 10 per cent without increasing fixed costs, what percentage impact will it have on net profit?' Operating leverage is calculated by dividing this percentage by 10 per cent.

First case

	Current (£)	Additional 10% (£)
Sales	100	110
Variable costs	90	99
Contribution	10	11
Fixed costs	0	0
Net profit	10	11 (an increase of 10%)

The operating leverage is 1, i.e. there is no leverage at all.

Second case

	Current (£)	Additional 10% (£)
Sales	100	110
Variable costs	60	66
Contribution	40	44
Fixed costs	30	30
Net profit	10	14 (an increase of 40%)

The operating leverage is 4.

Third case

	Current (£)	Additional 10% (£)
Sales	100	110
Variable costs	30	33
Contribution	70	77
Fixed costs	60	60
Net profit	10	17 (an increase of 70%)

The operating leverage is 7.

Fourth case

	Current (£)	Additional 10% (£)
Sales	100	110
Variable costs	0	0
Contribution	100	110
Fixed costs	90	90
Net profit	10	20 (an increase of 100%)

The operating leverage is 10.

I cannot leave leverage without mentioning the potential downside, even though it hardly fits into reaching for your dream. The upside potential of leverage is matched by the downside risk. If you have operating leverage of 5, then a 10 per cent improvement in your sales will produce a 50 per cent improvement in your profits. A 10 per cent drop in sales will produce five times that decrease in profits. If you have financial leverage, the downside is as dramatic as the benefit.

The impact of leverage has another dimension when you look at it in terms of dependency on customers. Suppose your biggest customer accounts for 20 per cent of your business, but, because of operating leverage, losing that sales turnover would wipe out your entire profit. It can easily be the case.

Operating at the margin

High street businesses generally have pretty high operating leverage. In fact, your target when running a restaurant should be for the gross margin on food to be about 65–70 per cent. Here's an example of what the profit-and-loss account might look like:

	Month 1	Month 2
Sales	10,000	11,000
Variable costs	3,000	3,300
Contribution	7,000	7,700
Fixed costs	6,000	6,000
Net profit	1,000	1,700

The increase of sales by 10 per cent gives a hugely disproportionate rise in profit. This gives a restaurant an operating leverage of 7.

In My Experience: Getting everyone to buy something

A girl I know runs a small art gallery. She took her hobby and managed to build it into a successful little business. The items she sells are mostly quite big ticket. She encourages browsers, and always has the door open so that people don't feel awkward when they leave without having bought anything.

After a while she bought in a stock of postcards, mainly of famous paintings. These she displayed around the gallery and, guess what, almost everyone bought one or more of them. They were, of course, inexpensive items, but funnily enough they had a very healthy margin. This was a very useful source of petty cash, as well as a method of encouraging people to feel comfortable in the gallery.

The rules that operating leverage teach us

Obviously you've got to know exactly what your fixed costs are and therefore your break-even point. (If you're unsure about break-even analysis, it's covered in Chapter 5.) Then you've got to know the variable cost of each item you sell. If you're selling gifts, then you will want to give a prominent display to items with a high mark-up. But you'll also want to display, near the till, some cheap products with a small margin but the potential for a high level of sales. What you're hoping is that a fair percentage of customers add the cheap knick-knack to what they've already bought.

It's easy to remember to keep the fixed costs as low as possible, after all it's up to you how many staff you have on and what you pay them. It can be slightly more difficult to lean equally heavily on variable costs. There are, for example, then salesmen for your suppliers who are constantly trying to improve their margins. Then there's the worry that, if you find a cheaper source of ingredients or whatever, you may damage the quality of the product and lose customers.

From the TV Series

Shopping around for ingredients

At Blue Vinny, Steve and Lindsay didn't shop around as hard as they might have for cheaper ingredients because it was easier to stay with their current supplier, and, anyway, Steve liked the way the salesman did business. Perhaps he would've thought twice about that decision if he'd worked out what his operating leverage was and realised the difference cheaper ingredients would make to the bottom line.

Keep people in your variable costs

As well as the positive leverage effect of having as few actual employers as possible, there are some other ways people can have a beneficial effect on leverage.

Firing poor performers is an expensive business, as is letting people go because you don't have the level of work for them that you were expecting. And don't underestimate the negative impact that this will have on morale. There is much less employee loyalty around now than there was in the past, mainly because of the behaviour of employers who, in reacting to very fast changes in the business environment, have shown themselves to be markedly less loyal to their staff. This means that people are more than willing to move to a competitor.

So, if you make wrong decisions in staffing, and have to put them right, you may find yourself with a morale problem which leads to the loss of the people you desperately need to keep.

One way out of this dilemma of 'Do we need another person and is this the right one?' is to use temps and contractors. (But be very careful of the tax position on contractors, especially in the IT business. The government is bearing down on contractors who use their employer's equipment and only have one customer. They regard such individuals as being, in reality, employees and want the tax and National Insurance contributions appropriate to that status.) Temps and contractors are not included in fixed costs. You can dispense with their services whenever you want and they are never regarded as full members of the team. This means that their departure is met with more equanimity than if they were permanent members of staff. The two disadvantages of this approach are the higher daily rate cost and the fact that you have no hold over these people. But remember, the more things you have in variable costs, the more efficient use you make of fixed costs and so leverage up the profits.

From the TV Series

Salary, what salary?

In normal circumstances, you'd have thought that the chief overhead in a hairdressing salon would be the wages of the stylists, but not at Loaf. Using all the charm and charisma that makes their project so exciting, and working for them so attractive, Richard and Craig have actually moved their staff into direct costs. They get no salary, but a commission on every customer they serve. This motivates the staff to get repeat business by being the best, and in addition makes them very interested in cross-selling the hairdressing products and treatments that they offer to customers.

By this strategy, the owners have lowered their overheads and got the break-even point down to a beautifully low level.

24 Keeping a wide and forward-looking perspective

At some point, you've got to stop diving in and solving short-term problems. And the best point at which to do it is right from the start.

What the business schools say...

Your washing machine is leaking. Finding the cause is not a complex process; you follow the water trail from where you saw it back to its source. It's a hose. It has frayed a bit and is obviously leaking, but not all the time, because when you got to it the machine was empty and the leak more or less dried up. You decide that the leak is very small and stick a bowl under the hose to catch the drips, vowing to check it from time to time and empty it if it's nearly full. Your decision is aimed at the effect. It has solved the problem with the least amount of effort and time. It could be that you will forget to empty the bowl and the floor will get wet again. It could also be that the unfixed leak will get worse until eventually the hose bursts and you have a major flood. But that is for the long term. Put differently, the bowl under the leak is minimising the effect, replacing the hose would be tackling the cause.

In an ideal world your business plan would be so good that you would be working solely on issues that have a high impact on your business performance but are of low urgency at the moment. In a less than ideal world, a lot of your activity will be spent on actions that not only have a high impact on the business but are also very urgent.

But...

Actually, the first bit of this is exactly right, I have no buts about it. They see the washing machine problem as 'cause and effect'; I prefer the terms 'fire-fighting and getting the business under control'. If you're always in fire-fighting mode there are two possibilities – it's a simple race between which dies first, the business or you.

As for the second part, I have to confess I work mainly on things that are fairly urgent; except, of course, the really big impact issues such as, 'Do I sell this property or buy another one?' And that's the problem. If you're always fire-fighting you never get round to the big issues; after all, you can put off implementing an expansion programme for ever, and no one will complain. But keep running out of stock of a good selling item and you'll see the customers voting with their feet.

Watch and learn

There's no point in risking it all if you're just going to be a full-time barman or hairdresser or whatever; that wasn't the realisation of your dream was it? Your aim is to build first a chain of outlets and then an empire. So think through very carefully your own contribution to the actual running of the outlets, particularly the first one. I'm not saying that you shouldn't be able to step in and help out with customer service or fetch things or even handle a problem with the plumbing. Indeed, I think it's vital to understand very thoroughly the jobs of the people who work for you. But try not to get involved in actually doing those jobs.

It's quite difficult to achieve. When something goes wrong, it's human nature to get busy solving the problem by handling the effect; but if everyone, including the owner, does that, then the problem is simply going to happen again.

Suppose one evening your restaurant is a waiter short; the easiest thing to say to whoever you have running the restaurant is, 'OK, I'll step in this time.' But beware, a number of negatives happen if you do that. Firstly, they will expect you to do it again and again, to the extent, probably, that you'll find yourself working every Tuesday evening. Next, at a stroke, you've taken away responsibility from whoever should've made sure that there were enough staff. Now they know that you'll just step in anyway. Thirdly, they haven't learnt how to handle a sudden resource problem; and even with the best systems and plans in the world, it's bound to happen again some time in the future. The answer is, just leave them to it. You'll be surprised how well they'll cope, and they'll probably enjoy the mini crisis and their solution to it.

Your job is to learn from the problem and work out what system needs to go in, what resource is required or what skill is lacking that caused the problem to occur in the first place. Step back and keep your wide perspective. After all, when this is a worldwide chain of restaurants, you won't be able to fly to New York every Tuesday to fill in for an absentee.

In My Experience: Keep your eyes peeled

I managed to obey this rule and built a multi-million pound pub company without ever going behind the bar. There were some very tempting moments in the early stages, but I kept my nerve.

I was, however, often in the bar, watching what was going on and looking at its strengths and weaknesses. I checked every day on what the first impression of the bar would be to a new customer. I talked to the customers, listened to their comments and tried to be as friendly as possible to encourage their return.

I learnt what people didn't like, so that I could get it put right. I learnt what people wanted, so that I could build it into my future plan, either for that particular outlet or another one. I kept my perspective, so that I could concentrate every day on what I needed to do to move the business forward. After all, no one else was going to do that for me.

Setting priorities

Now let's move on a step or two. You've got three outlets trading, plus you've got two premises being refurbished and made ready to open in about six weeks' time. You've also got the details on another six properties in your briefcase, all of which need to be read, and most of which you need to visit. And that's just the overview of what you have to do. You're very busy.

You've got an up-to-date list of actions that you have to get through, your in-tray is full of bumf and there are seventy emails in your inbox. Here's a quick method of setting priorities that I find useful when I need to make sure that I'm concentrating on the matters that have the most impact on the business, as opposed to those that are giving you the most pressure.

Put the paperwork, emails and actions into three categories A, B, and C, by assessing their urgency. Urgent is something that's got to be done now or it'll be too late. You get clues on urgency by looking at how much an item affects the profit-and-loss account and the future plan. Items that have a significant effect on other people always seem urgent, but stand back and check on their real importance.

A This is for stuff that you think is urgent, that you want to do today – things that you're going to deal with, even if it means missing out some other things. Generally speaking, you'll find matters to do with customers and customer satisfaction most likely to be in this category. Also in this category will be any contribution to a legal matter, such as a lease negotiation. These are very urgent, because if you take your time over them you've got no chance when they go back into the hands of the professionals. They can make even a simple legal exercise last for ever. This list becomes your target for the day; you really need to finish it off. If it's plainly impossible to do everything look for a holding operation on some that makes a bit of progress but takes relatively little time.

B This is stuff that's important but not as urgent as A. You'll get round to these today only if you finish with those in category A. Tomorrow, these matters could well go into A.

C The C pile may still be important, and you need to know where you've filed it, so that if something happens that changes its urgency you can promote the matter to A or B.

From the TV Series

Drowning in their own business

Paul and Lee in their café/bar in Burgess Hill signalled that they had a problem in this area when they described themselves using terms like 'glorified barmen'. One of them was working the bar at all times; often both of them were in there. They were so determined to get through the difficulties and make a success of their first idea that they didn't stand back and examine their strategy.

Tactically, it was dangerous too. If you work somewhere all the time you stop seeing the place as a customer sees it. When I went in one day there was a whole load of signboards and other stuff that they'd stored directly opposite the entrance to the bar. Perhaps the worst first impression they could give. But, like that bit of wood that you forgot to paint in the front hall and have just got used to, they'd got accustomed to the mess and didn't realise that there was anything wrong.

25 'I'm from the tax office, and I'm here to help'

Many businesspeople regard the tax and regulatory officers of government as 'the enemy'. But treat them well, and you'll be surprised how helpful they can be. Never be rude to anyone.

Look, you need help, so why not admit it?

The title of this chapter comes from the old large company joke, 'I'm from head office, and I'm here to help.' I've got some sympathy with this. Often the guys from head office are more interested in the centrally produced marketing strategy or the strict application of human resources rules than they are in whether or not the people in the field are satisfying a growing number of customers.

But I, and I've checked this with other people, find the opposite to be true when it comes to government agencies. OK, sometimes our planning rules can seem a little bit archaic and, dare I say it, inconsistent. And yes, the VAT inspector is not going to turn a blind eye to any small discrepancy. But in the main, these people are pro-business, want the economy to grow and will help anyone to understand, administer and play by tax and other regulations.

Now look at this matter from a civil servant's point of view. It's the nature of their role that they will interpret some rules in a way that doesn't suit all their clients. The planning officer may not think that the chairs and tables outside the bar in the pedestrian precinct are as unobtrusive as the guy trying to run the bar. And it is true that the VAT people will be more concerned about a payment being a few days late than your other creditors. These and other enforcements of the strict rule of law really get to a lot of people and they show it by becoming aggressive, rude and even abusive. But the civil servants have heard it all before. They are inured to angry clients on the telephone, deal with them and pass on. But they also have long memories.

Go out of your way to be nice to officials. Health and safety, planning, building regulations, tax, fire-fighters are all in a position to help or hinder you, and they're also all human beings. So, start from admitting you need their help. Human beings like to help people, especially if it involves displaying knowledge and expertise that the person they're helping doesn't have. Even when you are getting to understand the rules it is always a good idea to confess ignorance and seek guidance.

Call them by their names, go and visit them – not many people do that – and, dare I say it, schmooze them. Never ever be angry or show impatience. Never do anything that could possibly send them into their bunkers with a poor impression of you. That way, you'll be surprised just how helpful they can be. This strategy can also save you a lot of time, as they do things for you that otherwise you would have to work out for yourself. Forms are an excellent example of this. Filling out a form with the person whose job it is to read them takes a whole lot less time than doing it using the printed guide that comes with the form.

In My Experience: How to turn the planners against you, not to mention them next door

I know a man who owns a plot of land in the country. It is at the end of a triangular plot that already has three stone-built properties on it. He wants to build a stone house on the last plot, and, on the face of it, there's no reason in the world why he should not be allowed to.

But this is how he went about it. He applied to put up no less than four houses on the plot, on the grounds that they would scale it back to one or two. They didn't scale it back, they simply said 'No'. This overkill strategy also had the effect of turning the neighbours solidly against him.

He tried bullying the local officers. Then he harangued his councillor and any other councillor he could get hold of. He put in planning applications for fewer and fewer buildings over the next two years. In the end, he cut it down to one house and was confident that they would let that through. But his tirades, appeals against the rules and general obnoxiousness are likely to have done him no good. I believe that he will only get planning permission now if the current elected members and officials die, and all the neighbours move on. He should live so long.

But many people behave like this man. This gives you a huge opportunity to treat people properly and get what you want.

Everything you need to know about VAT – don't be afraid to ask

It's a bit more complex than this, but if you are going to have a sales turnover of more than a certain amount – at the moment it's roughly

£58,000 – you need to register and account for VAT. There is an excellent website at www.businesslink.gov.uk that will give you a lot of help. It's got step-by-step questionnaires to guide you through, from whether you need to register, to the forms and the other rules. Use this site by all means, but don't use it as a substitute for getting in touch with them. If it's geographically feasible, go and see them. If not, ring them up and ask for help. It'll pay off in the end.

The other big decision you have to make is when to account for VAT. You can do this at the time you raise an invoice or a supplier raises one to you. Or you can do it at the time the cash changes hands. This is an important decision that will affect your cashflow, so ask for help and make the right one.

In My Experience: It pays to go online

I've found three essential things that you must be able to use a computer well for in your dream business:

★ You must be able to write and print out professionally worded and looking letters.

★ You must be able to use a spreadsheet.

★ You must be able to get online and use the Internet for all the help it makes available at the click of a mouse.

This last one reaps a tangible benefit. Both the Inland Revenue and Customs and Excise, now, incidentally, joined into one institution, offer monetary rewards for filing things in online and doing other work using downloaded forms. The rewards change, but they're worth the effort, so make sure you have a look at what's available in that area.

Within 18 months to two years, you are very likely to get a VAT inspection. This involves one or two inspectors going through your books meticulously and in great detail. Prepare carefully for such an inspection. Give them a reasonable space to work in, rather than asking them to use a corner of your desk, or the kitchen table. Make sure your books are well organised and completely up to date.

Look after them. The smell of real coffee is a good welcome and provide biscuits, water and other hot drinks. They ain't going to miss anything they don't like, whatever you do, but it pays to treat them like the professionals they are. That's the key word to the relationship you're trying to create with them – professionalism. You're not trying to make them your friends, just dealing with them as business people.

From the TV Series

Paul and Lee and the outside terrace

It's good to balance what this chapter says with the other side of the coin. Officialdom does sometimes work rather slowly in the context of the dynamics of a new, and possibly struggling, venture. So in areas where there is no serious risk of getting into severe trouble always remember that it's easier to ask for forgiveness rather than for permission.

Paul and Lee wanted to put chairs and tables outside their café/bar. It was important, not only for the extra seating, but also to raise the profile of the café from the outside and improve the first impression that it offered people. They were waiting for planning permission until they realised that it was going to come through too late for their opening. So, they're entrepreneurs, what do you expect them to do? Naturally, they stuck the chairs and table on the pavement straightaway. After all, they can always ask for forgiveness if anyone complains.

26 Slowly dripping cash is like Chinese water torture

There is nothing worse than running a business at just about break-even. You can tinker away to your heart's content, but it's much wiser to take radical action before it's too late.

A radical change in direction does not mean that you've failed

OK, your dream is started. You've made the jump into your own business and done a lot of the difficult stuff. You've organised the builders, done the renovation and the concept is open to the public. The starting custom was lower than you had hoped, but has picked up a bit so that the revenue coming in each month more or less match the costs going out.

But you're not really making money, and you're certainly not making real money. This means that you are living on a very small salary, or none at all. And, of course, your life is not your own, it now belongs to the business. If you take your eye off the ball by, for example, having a day off to watch the school nativity play, the till will take less on a crucial day in the retailing year.

You work hard on improving things. You look at the competition to see what they're doing differently from you. You try to work out why their premises are busy all day long while you have lulls at different parts of the day. You get feedback from your customers by asking them what they like and dislike about the experience they've just had. Learning from all of this, you tune the look and feel of the premises and perhaps the products on offer. Trade goes up a bit, but you're still hovering round that break-even mark.

The question arises, 'At what point will you decide that the concept has a fundamental flaw, take a step back and replan your strategy?'

When to replan is when you're still in control of your business. I think there's a pivotal point in most small businesses after about six months. You haven't run out of money yet, but the accountant has drawn a graph showing you that you are within months of that happening. So, you're still in control. You could just wait the extra 12 months, watch the constant drip, drip, drip of cash going out and than have the bank step in and tell you what to do. When they do that, it almost certainly means you've risked it all and lost it all.

What the business schools say...

There is a general view out there that you haven't given a concept enough time until you've tried it for 12 to 18 months.

But...

Look at it more practically. Much earlier than that you've had warning signs. Suppose you realise after six months that break-even is still the best month that you ever have. Why wait another year? You're going to have lost even more money; and that's assuming you haven't had a heart attack or a nervous breakdown in the meantime. You're taking risks with your health and your family life, for goodness sake – and you haven't even got the compensation of pots of dough.

Look, you're a businessperson. In your heart of hearts, you'll know when you've tried everything and still not reached profitability. So don't hang about, have a radical rethink.

Stand back and think it through

Get away from the premises for a sensible amount of time to weigh up your position. List your strengths and weaknesses. Your strengths will include the fact that you've learnt a lot and gained valuable experience. You know how to organise builders, buy fixtures and fittings and design a retail concept. You've learnt how to hire, manage and fire staff, and you've learnt the technical part of your particular trade. You own the premises, or you have a lease on the premises, and you've improved them since you took over. You've still got a bit of cash in the bank.

Now look at the next crucial part of the planning process – your weaknesses. Look for a fundamental flaw. If it's the location, stop kidding yourself that somehow, as if by magic, it's going to improve. If it's the concept, admit it to yourself first of all, then to your friends and advisers.

Now look at your options. What could you do to overcome the weaknesses? Is there, for example, a skill that you lack that you could learn if you worked for someone else? Think radically, and then write down the options you've got. Talk to anyone who can help you to get away from your fixed idea of what you've being trying to do.

The first option is obviously to continue as you are, to keep tuning and to hope that things pick up. The others are more radical and probably involve a major change of direction.

It's decision-making time. Which of these options are you going with? Remember, a major change of direction is not an admission of failure; it's a decision to stop banging your head against a brick wall.

From the TV Series

A business at a pivotal point

Paul and Lee were at exactly this stage with their café/bar. They'd been in business for five or six months when their accountant told them that if things didn't improve they had two and a half months to go. They resolved to cut costs. This, of course, would make the personal side of the problem even worse. If you lose a member of staff to save money you have to work even more hours yourself.

Remember they were talking in terms of, 'We're not afraid of hard work. But it's taken over our lives completely. We've lost weight. We're always working. We have no social or sports life. We were prepared for a change in lifestyle but nothing like this. Anyone who thinks it's glamorous to own your own bar/restaurant business hasn't tried it yet...we haven't been able to change the people of Burgess Hill, who are set in their ways and not ready for a new sort of bar. We've become glorified barmen and waiters. And we're still not making money.'

So what were Paul and Lee's strengths? Much as the ones I list above, plus they knew how to run a kitchen. They'd learnt their products comprehensively and could advise customers confidently and accurately. And their relationship had stayed intact. (It's at this stage that a lot of people fall out with each other.)

In my view, they had a fundamental flaw in their premises. The bar was in the wrong place and it was simply too small for the business to succeed.

Paul, Lee and I agreed what their options were:

★ They could carry on as they were and hope for the best; perhaps asking an experienced bar designer to make some suggestions.

★ They could lease the premises to someone else and get a rent of about £30,000. This would give them a breathing space to find another bar to lease and do up. Once it was up and running they could lease that one and so on. They would become dealmakers rather than bar managers.

★ They could take the most radical decision of the lot and sell the freehold of the premises they'd vastly improved. Maybe it wasn't right for a bar; but other businesses have different characteristics and someone may well be interested in finding premises where they could avoid the stress and strains of renovation. This would release the capital they would need to lease or buy another facility in a better location, like a bigger town.

You see, it's always difficult to change people's buying habits. It's also much easier to lease or buy a going concern in the business you want to be in, than to start from scratch. And the real money lies with a progressive plan of growing the number of outlets rather than beavering away in the same place. After all, it's much easier to set up the second outlet than the first, the third is even easier than that, and so on.

In My Experience: Learn from your, and other people's mistakes

I wasn't born knowing about this, simple though it seems when you write it down. I learnt it because my first business only got to break-even point; I struggled on for 18 months and the business died a tortured death, slowly but surely dripping cash.

Part 5:
The X factor

Have you got what it takes to be an entrepreneur? There's something slightly special about successful ones. Have a think about what the X factor might be and examine yourself to see if you've got it, or how you can create it.

There's a big difference in running your own business and building up a chain of outlets managed by people you've hired in. I've tried to define this.

Chapter 27 It's a lot to do with taking risks and seeing the world from a different angle to other people. In the end it's common sense, but used, perhaps, in an uncommon way. I can see it in some businesspeople, but definitely not in others.

Chapter 28 It's a good section to remind ourselves that however great we may be as entrepreneurs, the paperwork still has to be done. Don't let it pile up and bog you down.

Chapter 29 Everyone knows it's going to be hard work risking it all, but have you thought through the implications chasing your dream will have on all aspects of your life?

Building a chain of outlets and eventually a national or even international brand is what entrepreneurship's all about. If you've got it what it takes you're going to have to go for it. It's what you're for.

27 What is the X factor?

Running a business and owning a chain of businesses as an entrepreneur are two very different things. There's an ingredient that's hard to define that separates the kind of person who can do the latter. It's the X factor of entrepreneurship.

What makes an entrepreneur?

Let's start with a dream, because you've got to have one. It may not be very long term; it's just something that you really want to make happen. Maybe it's as simple as, 'I dream of the day that I make enough money to be able to take a year off.' Then you need some ability to initiate an idea, to be the first to do something. Now you need a large dollop of determination. All of the people I know who have made it have had to battle through some pretty hard times, determined that it'll come right in the end. You need these attributes to set up and run your own business.

Now add what's necessary to be a successful entrepreneur rather than a successful business manager. Entrepreneurship is a lot about risk taking. Everyone in business knows that the greater the risk the greater the return, and entrepreneurs are likely to take far bigger risks. Take, for example, the vital aspect of finding a gap in the market. You're pretty sure it's there, you've done enough research to give you some confidence that it's a gap that you can exploit, and then you go for it. No ifs and buts. Just get on with it, because if you've spotted an opportunity you have a limited amount of time to exploit it before someone else spots the same one.

From the TV Series

Good news and bad news on the juice bar front

Sarah and Steve chose a location in Brighton for their juice bar. They could see the gap in the market and had some good reasons for thinking that they could fill it extremely well. The good news is that they've almost certainly been proved right – there is indeed an opportunity. One proof that they're right is the bad news – two other juice bars have opened up in the same area. It's certainly going to emphasise the other side of their reasons for going ahead – their quality and service – they're planning a great place to eat and drink and that's how they're going to win customers in such a competitive environment.

Have you got the 'nous' and self–confidence?

Here's a tricky bit of the entrepreneurial X factor to describe – I call it nous. Nous is the Greek word for the mind, and in English translates into common sense or gumption. To my mind, it's an innate know-how; it means that somehow you find the right route. To have nous, you've got to be bright. It doesn't mean you have to be terribly clever, you just have to be good at grasping things quickly, understanding how the world works and what your place in it could be.

Nous is not arrogance, but it's hard to talk about it without running the risk of sounding a bit arrogant. But anyway, here goes. Sometimes I simply can't believe how people can run their businesses in ways that are to me so obviously wrong. Quite honestly, some businesspeople appear to be pretty stupid. They're not stupid, I know that, but somehow they seem to be able, how do I describe it, to suspend their common sense and make startlingly bad decisions. Entrepreneurs don't do that. I find that entrepreneurs see as common sense what others don't see at all.

I've started up loads of new enterprises. When they were successful, it's interesting how often people have said to me, 'Well, it was a pretty obvious opportunity.' OK, maybe it was obvious, but no one else thought about filling that particular gap at that particular time.

From the TV Series

A gap in the children's entertainment market

When I first talked to Violaine of the Flying Fortress, I couldn't see the gap she was so certain that she'd identified. But it was there and she had the confidence and vision to see it and then fill it – a brilliant example of 'nous'.

Then there's self-confidence, over-riding self-confidence. You see the reflection of this in your ability to enthuse people about a new idea. You still seek advice, listen to and read about people with more experience than you, but, in the end, you have an aim and you never stop believing in your ability to achieve that aim.

Mao Tse-tung stole an army; can you believe that? He decided that an army would help him in his climb to the political top, knew that a small one was being raised not far away and simply went and took it over. Sir Freddie Laker started up selling second-hand aeroplane parts and ended up running an airline. Not only that, but his airline posed such a threat to the national flag carrier airlines that several countries had to bend the rules, that is cheat, in order to drive him out of business. I could go on. There are many people who have similarly made things happen. People do achieve incredible feats, and one of the things that lumps them together is that they thought of the incredible thing and knew that they, and only they, could do it.

Part of nous is to have good intuition about people and how they behave. It's the ability to empathise and imagine what your employees and customers will think about something. This empathy suggests a path. I go down this path in my head, and ask myself what others will make of it, trying at all times to be completely honest with myself. When I've run the model through my head a few times, and am sure that the opportunity is both real and better than what other people are doing, the time has come to get going.

In My Experience: Talk about the good news and keep the bad to yourself

People like dealing with winners. They prefer to buy where other people are buying; they like to feel as though they're up with the trends and, for example, eating and drinking in popular places. For this reason, it's important to talk your business up at all times. Keep a very positive attitude as you talk to your friends, customers and suppliers. Tell them you're enjoying growing the business and that people are starting to become customers at a good rate. If you're plainly not very busy, tell them that you're on the business plan and confident that you'll stay there.

Allied to this is – never look desperate. If things get tough, for example, there's a temptation to lower prices to push up sales. This can be a slippery slope if customers sense desperation. The increase in sales might not happen if they start to avoid your business because they think you're in trouble. Besides, you're making a lower contribution from sales since your variable costs have stayed the same, so you need even more customers to cover your fixed costs.

I learnt this lesson the hard way. One of my restaurants wasn't doing too well, so we put promotion girls outside handing out discount vouchers. The restaurant became even quieter, since potential customers thought that there must be something wrong with a restaurant that had to do something so desperate. Look for promotions that add value to your business rather than underselling it.

What the business schools say...

The business schools teach entrepreneurship and there is a current thought that it should be taught in schools. The theory is that you encourage people to think differently about business if they've been brought up doing exercises that make them think like an entrepreneur.

WHAT IS THE X FACTOR? **215**

But...

I'm not sure that you can teach entrepreneurship in business school.
Perhaps you can show people how to exploit their entrepreneurial
skills, but if they haven't got it, they haven't got it. I must say, however,
that I warm to the thought of talking to young children about it at
school. Most entrepreneurs do start pretty young, and children haven't
yet learnt to be terrified of taking a risk.

28 Keep on top of the dull stuff

The exciting part of running a business is the planning of it and putting the plan into action. The dull stuff is the administration. Here are some thoughts on types of trader, and tips on not getting bogged down in the paperwork.

Don't put off the paperwork

If you let the admin build up it gets worse. Why? Because you keep having to go through the learning process of working out how to do it again and again. So, if you're keeping your own books, do it regularly, and don't let it slip until it looks extremely hard to do. Accounts that are two months old become impossible to decipher and take three times the time and cost to sort them out. The best way is to set aside a certain amount of time on a regular basis. Well, what else are evenings and weekends for?

In My Experience: Here's a good challenge

I got this piece of advice from a well-organised person. It's very simple to say, but pretty tricky to carry out. But it's worth aiming at. It goes:

'Never handle a piece of paperwork twice.'

The suggestion is that, when you settle down to do your emails, or when you open the post, you make sure you've got enough time to take action as well as just read the contents. You should try to deal with each document there and then. It's difficult, I know, and no one can completely avoid putting a document into an in-tray for later attention. But if you try to carry out the 'only handle it once rule' you'll definitely reap some benefits.

Firstly, you'll find that the jobs you would normally have put off are, when you try to deal with them immediately, actually much easier to solve than you thought. Secondly, you'll find that, if you're determined not to come back to the document, but you're not sure what to do about it, the rule makes you take an action, like sending a note to your accountant or whatever, that starts the ball rolling to handle the issue in the end. Thirdly, you'll get a reputation with your suppliers, customers and others of being professional. And everyone likes dealing with a professional.

Try it for a week and see how you get on.

I know it's not just me, because I've talked to other people about it. They agree that one of the best examples of this getting harder and harder business is your income tax return. If you do your own tax return, do it when it comes in. All you have to do is gather the relevant documents, like the annual tax statement for each of your bank accounts and so on, and then go through the form. It's not that difficult actually, and if you do hit a problem a call to the Inland Revenue will give you an instant answer every time. The fact is that you've got to do it at some point, and you're much more likely to remember where the data is if you do it at the beginning of May than if you leave it to the end of January.

The same goes if you get your accountant to do your return. The difference is that they will send you an annual letter telling you what they need to complete the return. Same thing goes, do it straightaway, when the letter comes in.

What the business schools say...

Business schools teach you everything you need to know to be able to do your own books, VAT returns and so forth. You probably have to sit an exam on it.

But...

The only thing is that it is very broad and general; in many ways you learn too much. When you go out on your own, resolve to find out just enough to be able to do your own work.

There's another balance to be found here. If you do all the admin yourself, then you've got to spend quite a bit of time learning how to do it and then actually doing it. Remember, you've got to be able to do it properly; PAYE, NIC and VAT have to be accounted for and paid on time or you'll get into lots of strife. Doing it yourself can save a lot of money; bookkeepers and accountants cost a fair amount. But there's another issue here. I tend to want to be able to do anything in the business that someone else can do. So I suppose my general advice would be to do it at the start, get the hang of it and then, when there is some income to pay for it, get professional help.

Incidentally, I'm afraid it's just not feasible to run a business without being able to work with computer spreadsheets. If, for some reason, you don't have this skill, then http://catalogue.learndirect.co.uk will give you directions on finding a suitable teach yourself package. There are lots of other sites too, just Google 'learn spreadsheets'.

And while I'm on about the dull stuff...

Try not to spend too much time worrying over the status of the trading company you are setting up. Normally it's pretty straightforward. If, for example, you're going to put in a lot of capital and hire a load of people you will want to be a limited company. Otherwise, you will want to be a sole trader or partnership. You have to check the tax situation and decide accordingly. A partnership can be very tax efficient if you are setting up a business that involves your partner in life. A partnership also gives you the opportunity to raise money. You can bring in another partner, who has to put in some capital to buy themselves into the partnership.

If you are a sole trader, just about your only source of funds is your banker, or possibly your friends and family, since, of course, anyone else who puts money in would want shares in partnership or limited company form.

The choice for raising funds is much wider if you are a limited company, but there is more paperwork and expense involved in keeping up with the red tape.

Setting up as a sole trader

★ Tell your local tax inspector and Contributions Agency. You'll be surprised how helpful these people can be, plus they have loads of brochures that cover most people's situations.

★ Make sure there is no planning problem with starting a business in the location you have chosen.

★ If you give your business a different name from your own, don't forget to include your name somewhere on your headed notepaper.

★ Decide, probably by talking to the VAT office, whether or not you need to register for VAT. Do it online (see Chapter 25).

Setting up as a partnership

The only drawback of a partnership is that each partner is jointly liable for the debts of the partnership. This means that if there is trouble, no matter who caused it, your assets, including your home if you own it, are at risk. This means that the degree of trust required in a partnership is very high indeed. Even with your life partner, some would say, never have an informal partnership arrangement. It is relatively easy to get a general partnership agreement that fits your case. If you can't find something that fits your needs, you may have to explain what you want to a lawyer and pay for a tailored agreement.

Think ahead and make sure that the agreement covers any eventuality. Make sure the agreement describes in detail how the business will be managed and controlled.

Setting up a limited company

Get a starter pack from Companies House. The easiest way to set up a limited company is to buy one off the shelf from a company formation specialist. To set up a private limited company you need one director and a company secretary, who cannot be the sole director. You can start such a company with very little capital indeed. The starter pack tells you what forms and fees to send.

When you are setting up a company, the important issue is to get started producing and selling your products and services. For this reason, it is likely that you will benefit from using an accountant who will take you through the processes and tell you, for example, what meetings to convene and what resolutions to pass.

You don't need to go far to find all the information and advice you need in this area. Here are some websites that could help:

Sole trader:
http://www.bytestart.co.uk/content/19/19 1/what-is-a-sole-trader.shtml

Partnership:
http://www.businesslink.gov.uk/bdotg/action/layer?topicId=1073864308

Limited company:
http://www.businesslink.gov.uk

All:
http://www.startups.co.uk/Yb62e40.html
and www.companieshouse.gov.uk

The dull stuff can go horribly wrong

I hate to bring in a touch of rancour here, but don't believe that fraud can't happen to you. In the experience of the people I have talked to, and in my own experience, fraud is rare. Most people live reasonably honest lives. This means that if fraud does affect you it is all the more surprising and dispiriting.

A bloke I know got into bad trouble as the result of a partner fiddling the books in his partnership. Being pretty knowledgeable in the bookkeeping admin area he got away with it for a long time until a big VAT inspection.

There's another way that a trusted person can dupe you. The son of one of the highly trustworthy key people in a growing cleaning firm was put in charge of the mailroom. The son made money on the side by systematically changing the values on invoices and pocketing the difference. Actually, it didn't last long since he omitted to alter the VAT total pro rata.

So, it can happen. Guard against it and insure against it if necessary. The key, at the planning stage of everything, is to put in watertight safeguards. They may seem like a sledgehammer to crack a nut, but in five years' time they may turn out to be a very necessary procedure.

I know an investment club with 20 members. When they wrote the original rules, they insisted that four people, one of whom is not the treasurer, were required to sign a cheque of any size. 'Anyone would think there was hundreds of thousands of pounds at stake here,' grumbled one member who thought, because the fund scarcely exceeded £2000, they were overdoing it. He doesn't grumble now that the fund is worth quarter of a million.

Be sensible, trust people, but get the security of formal agreements round you at all times.

Anyway, for goodness sake, enough of the dull stuff; let's go on to another, more interesting topic.

29 Just do it – if you're tough enough

As you grow your business, you'll meet a number of hurdles. Some of these concern the law, and many concern officialdom. Officials are mainly nice people, who need to be well treated, but they do have more time to go through the motions than you do.

Ask for forgiveness rather than permission

I've talked about entrepreneurship being about taking a few risks. The simple idea in this chapter is that you have to take a few risks with officials or they'll slow you down and possibly hammer your business.

Take planning permission. It's a good idea to have rules of planning, and I don't think anyone should flout them. But sometimes, if you're pretty sure you're going to get planning permission to do something, just do it. If you're wrong, and they eventually decide that what you're doing doesn't fit the rules and regulations, you can always ask for forgiveness. If you can then show how undoing what you've done will kill your business, they'll probably find some compromise that just obeys the rules, makes you have to make some minor changes, but leaves you with the business intact.

It's the same with paying your suppliers. You've got to pay your regular suppliers because they have the ultimate sanction – they can stop supplying you. I also believe it's a good idea to pay small and local companies quickly, because it builds good will and, who knows, it might create customers. But for the rest, when you're just getting started, they have to get in the queue. If they don't bully or threaten you and you can get a bit of free credit by not paying them, then my opinion is – just do it.

In My Experience: Flyposting

Flyposting is an occupational hazard in the pub and club trade. If you don't do it you're missing out on customers, but if you do do it you may be breaking the law. First of all, never ask if you're breaking the law, it's better to ask for forgiveness. Sometimes, forgiveness comes in the shape of a punishment, and one time I did get fined for flyposting. But I'm afraid that the business we got from the publicity was worth more than the fine.

I know a man who runs a contracting firm in the building industry and he protects his cashflow by writing the cheques at the time when he is due to pay the bills, but doesn't send them out until the creditors have rung him up a couple of times. When they complain he apologises like anything.

If you deal with big companies, managers may well tell you not to talk to the level above them. 'If you talk to my boss, I'll make sure you never do any business with this company again,' they say. Well, you've got to make a judgement. I've found that the higher up the organisation you talk, the more business you do; so this is a really good illustration of what this chapter is about. Never ask anyone if you may talk to their boss, their friends or anyone else who may become a customer. Just do it. After all if you ask for permission they may say 'No'.

So, you think you're tough enough...

Doing things that you know are going to upset some people or bring down the wrath of officialdom takes courage. But it's a hard world, the world of new businesses, and you have to ask yourself if you're tough enough. Are you mentally tough enough? Or do you feel better with the security of a large company behind you?

Can you ask your family to do without things? It's not easy to tell your partner that they can no longer afford something until your business has grown. Will they do without the gym membership? Will they forego holidays for the duration? Will they settle for carboot clothes for the kids? It puts a considerable stress on the family, so make sure that everyone is tough enough.

Are you physically tough enough? You're going to spend a lot of time working and very little time looking after yourself. You'll be eating on the move, drinking more than's good for you and smoking twice as much as you did before, or whatever your vice is. You're going to be tired and the family will have to put up with a bit more rudeness and irritability than they did before.

And then there are the customers – they're unreasonable, but they're always right. They get angry, sometimes with justification, often without. They don't always tell the truth and they have you in their power. Their word to other customers is terribly important to you and they know it. So, you've got to be tough enough to deal with them and keep smiling.

At the same time as dealing with difficult situations and a hard lifestyle, you're also trying to keep your eye on the ball and make the business fly. It's tough, you can't deny it.

What the business schools say...

If an employee signs a contract, then it's reasonable for the supplier who has that signed contract to assume that the person signing had the authority to do so. The contract is good.

But...

Sometimes the permission/forgiveness boot is on the other foot. I'll tell you what some salespeople do. They wander into your premises when there's only a very junior or even temporary member of staff there, and get them to sign a contract for changing your electricity supplier, ordering 'essential' fire extinguishers or advertising in some new directory that's coming out shortly, or whatever. I renege on such contracts and have never lost an argument with a supplier whose representative has behaved like that.

Having said all this, keep it all in perspective. Running your own show and bringing off the task of building a successful business is a massive boost to your self-esteem and confidence; so battling with officialdom and dealing with the hard knocks that come your way are, in the end, absolutely worth it.

Conclusion: Are you going to take the plunge?

OK, you've read the book, I wonder if you should put it all into practice, like now. Ask yourself if this is the right time to throw off the chains of nine-to-five drudgery. Shouldn't you stop selling your labour to someone who looks a lot more prosperous than you? If you've got a good idea and a plan to implement it, why not give it a go?

Here's your checklist

Run through in your mind the five vital areas to get right before you dive in:

0 You've checked that it's a **viable** idea by looking hard at the local competition and asking friends, family and particularly enemies what they think. You've learnt a lot from the people who spotted the flaws in your plan and listened hard to everyone's feedback. You've thought about the lifestyle, agreed it's worth a go with the people close to you and got yourself a good person to bounce ideas off. All of that and you still believe passionately that it's a runner. Well done, climb to the board that's five metres above the water.

5 You've checked your **motivation**. It's not just the huge pleasure of going to the bosses and telling them that you've decided to move

on and get rich; yes, everyone enjoys doing that. But there's a positive motivation there as well. You really want to run your own business. Not only that but you know the sort of business you want to run because you'll love it. You've thought about work/life balance, admitted that it's going to suffer badly for a while, but if you keep to the plan it'll improve to an acceptable level in an acceptable amount of time. Up the ladder again and pause at ten metres.

10 You've got the **skills** you absolutely must have before you start. You also know yourself well enough to recognise the ones you're going to have to work on. Where you really have a deficiency, you know who's going to plug the gap. The one skill you've cracked is having a clear picture in your head of your completed premises. And the first impression customers will get is absolutely fantastic. Your target market is going love it. Take a deep breath, go up the next ladder and think about money.

15 At fifteen metres the air is a little thin and people are using unfamiliar jargon. But you've mastered enough of it to find out who's got the **money** you need to get going. You understand cashflow, you've polished up your negotiating skills and you've thought through the implications of borrowing money. You also know the pitfalls of borrowing from people who right now are your friends and family. Good, your plan is going well and you're getting nearer the moment of truth. Go to twenty metres.

20 If I were you I wouldn't look down yet. There's one more checklist to go through before you do that. Do you know the difference between an entrepreneur's **x factor** and a business manager? Which one are you? Can you handle the dull stuff – you know the paperwork and bureaucratic red tape? And finally, come on, don't mess me about, are you tough enough? Yes to all of these? Well done, you've cracked it. You've done your preparation and you're at the edge of the highest board. It's time to look down.

Hey, what are you waiting for? Come on in, the water's **terrifying**.

Also available from Random House

PERFECT CV

Max Eggert

Whether you're applying for your first job or planning an all-important career move, your CV is the most potent strike weapon in your armoury. This classic, bestselling book is a concise and invaluable guide that gives you the blueprint for the perfect CV. It shows you clearly and quickly how to present you and your skills and experience in the best possible way – and how to avoid the many easily-made mistakes which swiftly antagonize potential employers.

Chapters include:

What to include – and exclude
Structures that work for you
Making your CV say 'see me'
Presenting yourself in a unique way
Creating the right image
50 tips and strategies

The author Max Eggert is a psychologist and international consultant specialising in human resource management, interim management and outplacement.

PERFECT LEADER

Andrew Leigh and Michael Maynard

The Perfect Guide To Unleashing Your Leadership Potential

Are leaders born or made? *Perfect Leader* shows clearly how everybody can learn to exercise leadership. The book is comprehensive, yet concise and to the point. It is written in clear language and is designed to be of immediate, practical benefit to readers. It explains exactly what it takes to be a leader by identifying and examining the seven 'I's of leadership:

Insight
Initiative
Inspiration
Involvement
Improvisation
Individuality
Implementation

Today's business methods, with their emphasis on teamwork, and on fewer layers of management, mean that there is a need for effective leaders to bring about corporate success – and in the process build themselves a satisfying career.

The authors Andrew Leigh and Michael Maynard run Maynard Leigh Associates, the human resources and development consultancy.

WALKING THE TALK

Carolyn Taylor

The culture of an organisation can mean the difference between success and failure. Leaders cast long cultural shadows, and if you want to positively change corporate culture, you have to walk the talk. This book shows you how.

Carolyn Taylor provides a groundbreaking guide to all aspects of building an effective culture, showing readers how to lead, define, plan, analyse and capitalise on culture to transform themselves and their organisations.

Walking the Talk covers everything from measuring culture to changing people's behaviour (including your own) and describes in detail five cultures which deliver great results: *Achievement*, *Customer-Centric*, *One-Team*, *Learning and People-First*.

BOO HOO

Ernst Malmsten, Erik Portanger & Charles Drazin

$135 million, 18 months...a dot.com story
from concept to catastrophe

A gripping, insider's account of the rise and fall of this most controversial of internet startups – a global, online retailer of sports and designer clothes.

'Such a dazzling version of the boo phenomenon that as readers turn the pages they will be rooting for the company to survive even though they know the story ends in disaster.'
Sunday Times

'*boo hoo* is an engrossing account of how two childhood friends per-suaded some of the world's savviest investors and fashion houses – including Bernard Arnault's LVMH and the Benetton family – to fund a sports and designer clothing company to the tune of $100m.'
Guardian

'One of the hottest books on the shelves at Waterstones.'
Sunday Times Style magazine

'Reading [this] has the fascination of watching a high-speed car crash replayed in slow motion. You know what's going to happen, you can see the confident glow on the drivers' faces, but can't warn them about the curve in the road that is coming to unstick them. Schadenfreude is irresistible. And yet everyone walks away unhurt.'
Independent

NATURAL BORN WINNERS:

HOW TO ACHIEVE YOUR AMBITIONS
AND CREATE THE SUCCESS YOU WANT

Robin Sieger

'Sometimes life can seem so unfair. You work hard, you do your best – but nothing seems to change. And yet there are others who, with the effortless ease of angels, always seem to get what they want. Why?'

We are all Natural Born Winners – but although we're born with the ability to succeed, it can often be lost in early childhood. Robin Sieger shows how that ability can be rediscovered with ease and immediately put to use in the pursuit of both personal and professional goals. The principles governing success are constant – and you can learn them.

Thousands of people have been spurred on to greater success through the inspiring principles of *Natural Born Winners*, published around the world in five languages. With this remarkable and inspiring book as your guide, you can share in their success, and rediscover the Natural Born Winner in you.

GETTING TO YES

William Ury & Roger Fisher

With over 2 million copies sold in over 20 different languages,
Getting to Yes *is the most successful book on Negotiation on the*
market!

Negotiation is a way of life for the majority of us. Whether we're at work, at home or simply going out, we want to participate in the decisions that affect us. Nowadays, hardly anyone gets through the day without a single negotiation, yet, few of us are armed with the effective, powerful negotiating skills that prevent stubborn haggling and ensure mutual problem-solving.

Fisher and Ury cut through the jargon to present a few easily remembered principles that will guide you to success, no matter what the other side does or whatever dirty tricks they resort to.

They include:

Don't bargain over positions
Separate people from the problem
Insist on objective criteria
What if they won't play?

THE COMING COLLAPSE OF CHINA

Gordon G. Chang

'Passionately polemic'
Observer

The world sees a glorious future for China. Beneath the veneer of modernization however, it's another story. *The Coming Collapse of China* predicts the imminent implosion of the economy and government of the People's Republic of China.

'*The Coming Collapse of China* does not flinch. It states what almost no one will say out loud: the end of the modern Chinese state is near. The People's Republic has five years, perhaps ten, before it falls. This book tells why'

Amazon.co.uk

'Chang's apocalyptic chapters diagnose and forecast the far-reaching, destabilizing effects of ongoing economic crisis on Chinese society and politics'

Observer

'Damning data and persuasive arguments that should set some Communist knees a-knocking'

Kirkus Reviews

GOOD TO GREAT

Jim Collins

'*Good to Great* is the best new business book I have read this year.'
Management Today

In 1996, Jim Collins and his research team set out to answer one simple question: 'Can a good company become a great company and, if so, how?' Most great companies grew up with superb parents who instilled the seeds of greatness early on. But what about the vast majority of companies that wake up part way through life and realise that they're good, but not great?

With 21 research associates working in groups of four to six at a time, over a period of nearly five years, the study examined 1,435 Fortune 500 companies at a cost of c. $500,000. The findings and concepts produced are counter-intuitive – and rigorously supported by the evidence.

'There is nothing to touch Jim Collins's *Good to Great* which isolates the characteristics that can turn a good company into a great one. It is essential reading.' *Sunday Times*

'Collins has, once again written an important book at the right time. He has set a stirring challenge to all managers: is "good" good enough? Or do you really want – and need – to be great?' *Business Voice*

'The boards of M&S, Marconi and BT would do well to read this book.'
Observer

Order further Business Books titles
from your local bookshop, or have them delivered
direct to your door by Bookpost

☐ **Perfect CV** Max Eggert	1844131440	£6.99
☐ **Perfect Leader** Leigh & Maynard	1844138070	£6.99
☐ **Walking the Talk** Carolyn Taylor	1844131483	£12.99
☐ **Boo Hoo** Malmsten, Portanger & Drazin	0099418371	£7.99
☐ **Natural Born Winners** Robin Sieger	0099476673	£9.99
☐ **Getting to Yes** Ury & Fisher	1844131467	£8.99
☐ **Coming Collapse of China** Gordon G. Chang	0099445344	£8.99
☐ **Good to Great** Jim Collins	0712676090	£20

Free post and packing
Overseas customers allow £2 per paperback

Phone: 01624 677237

Post: Random House Books
c/o Bookpost, PO Box 29, Douglas, Isle of Man IM99 1BQ

Fax: 01624 670923

email: bookshop@enterprise.net

Cheques (payable to Bookpost) and credit cards accepted

Prices and availability subject to change without notice.
Allow 28 days for delivery.
When placing your order, please state if you do not wish to receive any
additional information.

www.randomhouse.co.uk/arrowbooks